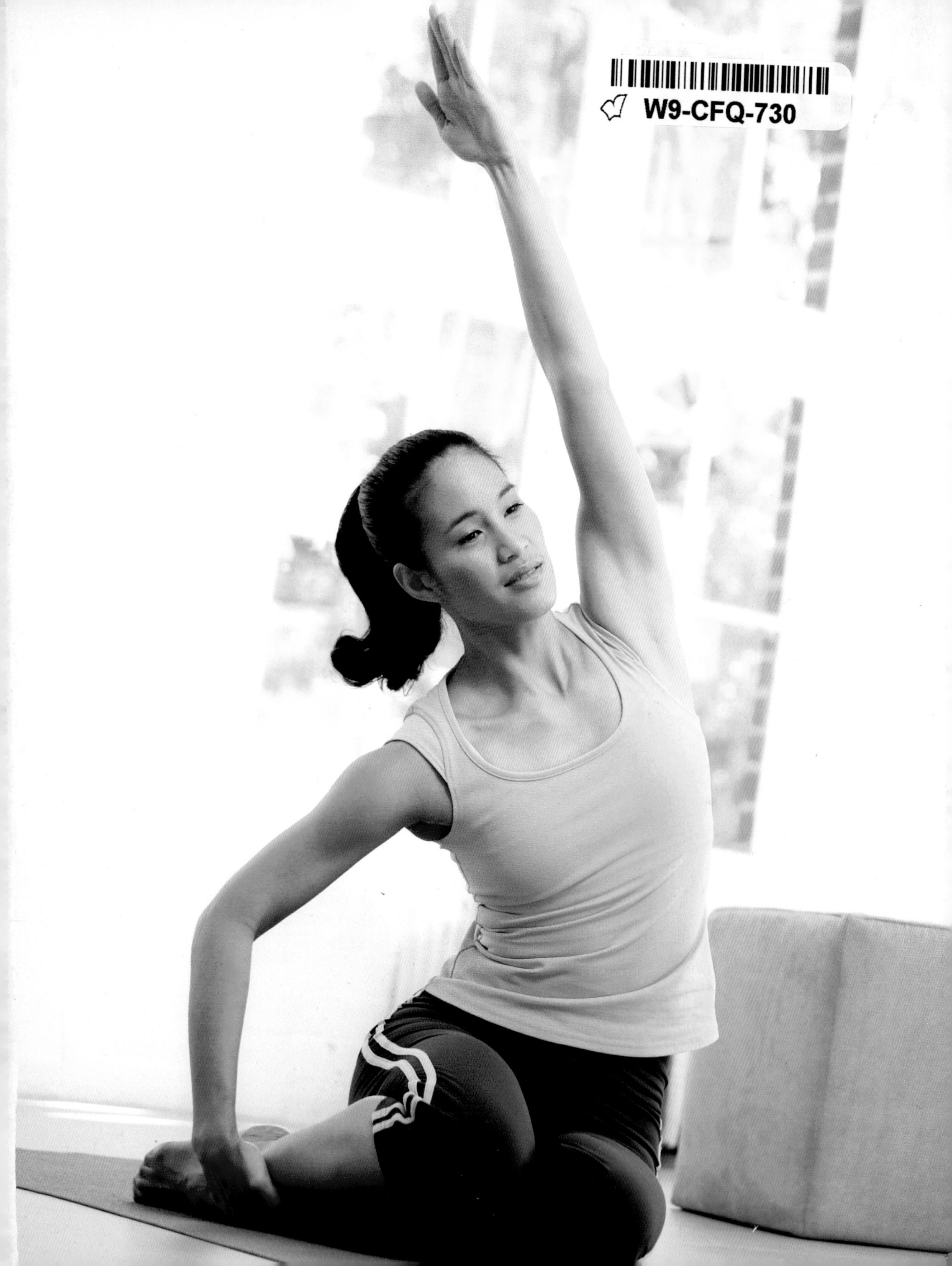

>> **15** minute
STRETCHING
& PILATES

SUZANNE MARTIN
& ALYCEA UNGARO

contents

>> **15**minute

STRETCHING

WORKOUT

author foreword

Here it is! Thanks to all of you who enjoyed my first Stretching book, and especially, to all of you who contacted me to request more Stretching and succeeded in exerting your influence in spurring the production of this book. Here are four themes with stretches that have been a part of my regimen for years. A special welcome to those of you new to stretching. May you become a lifelong convert!

Stretching is an integral part of body maintenance, as essential as brushing your teeth. Please don't be misled into thinking of it as a competitive sport, where more is better. This is not the case. Stretching is for everyone, male or female, naturally flexible or uncomfortably stiff. Correct stretching changes how your whole body looks, as well as providing pain relief and reducing stress.

Keep your mind open. Some of the instructions given may seem prescriptive, but that is because the effectiveness of the stretches lies in the set-up. Many people spend years in the gym, yet never seem to gain results. They don't pay attention to their set-up.

Look hard at the pictures and tips. The explanations will help you to organize the exercise concepts in your mind, which will help you to organize the efforts in your body to gain the greatest effect. This may take time, so be patient.

The stretches will reveal where your body needs help.
Observe and compare one side of your body to the other. Can
you feel both sides "organizing themselves" into the movement or
position? Is any body part talking to you? Please remember that
our supple models are only demonstrators. Follow the instructions,
mimic the basic shapes, and understand the cues. Then take the
movements farther. Internalize them until you can feel every bone
inside your body. Learn to compare the way your body stretches
today to the way it stretched yesterday. Don't compare it with the
model's body.

Learn to see your body as it is. The famous composer
Stravinsky once said that once he knew his limitations, then
he could become creative. Until we see our bodies as they really
are, and respect their individuality, we won't bring about change.

Take the challenge. Construct a new, improved you. These
simple exercises hold a key to your body's potential. Permanent
change happens one little increment at a time. Each 15-minute
segment will bring you closer to a more wonderful you. Enjoy.

Dr. Suzanne Martin

>> **how to use** this book

Stretch toward a new you! Each of the four programs in this book uses stretching to develop different aspects of your body. Think of those aspects like the facets of a diamond, honed with precision by the diamond cutter so each one sparkles and makes a glorious whole.

This book shows you how to transform your body—and your life—through stretching. Each stretch can stand by itself, but when done in sequence, you will experience a powerful cumulative effect. To start, read the introduction to each program to get an idea of its theme. Then watch the demonstration on the DVD, which demonstrates all four programs and is designed to be used with the book. As you watch, page references to the book flash up on the screen. Refer to these for more detailed instruction.

Next, try the program for yourself, then read the FAQs pages and annotations, and study the "feel-it-here" patches on the exercise pages to learn more and make the moves more your own.

Certain stretches will be harder for some people than for others, depending upon experience and body type. Remember, there's always an easier way to get into a harder move, so use the modification suggestions in the FAQs pages and on pp118–119. Remember, too, that you need to do a variety of motions in many different planes in order to identify weak links in your body.

There's no such thing as an easy exercise. Any exercise or stretch, however simple it may seem, brings greater benefits the more mindfully you do it.

The gatefolds

The gatefolds help you see each stretch sequence as a whole. Once you've watched the DVD, and examined the modifications and tips for each exercise, the gatefold will help reinforce the sense of the sequence and gives you a quick at-a-glance

reference. More importantly, when working without the DVD, you can also use the gatefold to prolong a stretch and linger from stretch to stretch, embellishing and savoring each as times permits.

Safety issues

Be sure to get permission from your healthcare provider prior to beginning a new exercise program. The advice and exercises are not intended to be a substitute for individual medical help.

wake up the stretch at a glance

1 ▲ **Energizing** Hand pull, page 24   2 ▲ **Energizing** Hand pull, page 24   3 ▲ **Limbering** Elbow circles, page 25   4 ▲ **Limbering** Elbow circles, page 25

13 ▲ **Balancing** Seated cross-leg twist, page 30   14 ▲ **Balancing** Seated cross-leg twist, page 30   15 ▲ **Elongating** Shoulder wedge, page 31   16 ▲ **Elongating** Shoulder wedge, page 31

At-a-glance gatefolds demonstrate the flow of each program, providing a quick reference so you can perform a neat, succinct, 15-minute sequence.

9 **Hurdler lat stretch** Come to a sitting position with both legs comfortably out to the sides. Tuck one foot in toward the groin and reach both hands over toward the extended leg. Sit evenly on your sitbones. Hold wherever it feels comfortable, either at the knee or lower down if you can. Bring both shoulders parallel to the floor. Breathe in, round into your back, and lower your head. Resist the stretch by holding firmly with the hands, on the outside of the leg.

tuck the pelvis under

10 Exhale, pull forward with your hands, round the back even more, and look toward your navel. Repeat 2 more times, then release your hands, roll your shoulders, and repeat on the other side.

feel it here

pull

press the calf down

>> posture stretch

11 **Balance point stretch** Remain sitting. Bend your knees, slide a hand underneath each thigh, and lift your feet off the floor, finding your point of balance. You will probably need to lean back a little. Use padding underneath your bottom if you need it. Roll your shoulder blades down the back and pull with your arms to hold yourself up. Inhale and bow your head, rounding your back.

feel it here

12 Squeeze your sitbones together and pull down on your arms. Sit tall and lift your groin muscles toward your head. Repeat 5 more times, breathing in as you round, and exhaling as you sit tall.

pull and lift

posture stretch >>

"Feel-it-here" patches in some of the illustrations to the steps reveal the particular areas of your body that the stretch is working on—and where you are most likely to feel the benefits.

annotations provide extra cues, tips, and insights

the gatefold shows all the exercises in the program

Rib breath, page 26

6 ▲ **Articulating** Rib breath, page 26

7 ▲ **Coordinating** Side reach, page 27

8 ▲ **Coordinating** Side reach, page 27

9 ▲ **Lengthening** Lift & bow, page 28

10 ▲ **Lengthening** Lift & bow, page 28

11 ▲ **Opening** Seated cat, page 29

12 ▲ **Opening** Seated cat, page 29

▲ **Coordinating** Alligator/Cat, page 32

18

19 ▲ **Opening** Arm fans, page 33

20 ▲ **Opening** Arm fans, page 33

21 ▲ **Powering** Modified cobra, page 34

22 ▲ **Powering** Modified cobra, page 34

23 ▲ **Lengthening** Shoulder ovals, page 35

24 ▲ **Lengthening** Shoulder ovals, page 35

>> **defining** the stretch

Welcome to the world of stretching. Not only will you come across many stretches, you will also find many types of stretches. Forget all those preconceived notions about the value of holding a stretch for an indefinite amount of time. Let these stretches move you.

There's more than one way to stretch. That's because there's more to it than simply stretching muscles. Arteries, veins, and nerves that supply the muscles are involved, too. What is also important is the stretch of the fascia—the connective tissue that permeates the whole body and wraps around the muscles and holds them close to the skeleton.

Think of it as a biomechanical "architecture." The bones are the scaffolding and the fascia is the bricks and mortar that support the volume of the structure. The fascia adapts to its environment. If you were put into a small closet and forced to sit in a crouched position for days on end, over time your body would attempt to shrink to fit into the extreme environment. The fascia does the same.

Compensating for bad habits

Our bodies are remarkably forgiving because we still function, even with poor posture—rounded shoulders and a forward head, or a protruding belly or collapsing ankles. The body compensates for weaknesses or faulty habits, but the compensations become "solidified," altering the patterns of our fascia and muscles. For this reason, we need different types of stretching to reverse any tightening to which our body has become accustomed.

Stretching strategies

We also need different stretches to address the properties of the various parts of our body. Moving stretches where, for instance, the head is rotating, the knee is bending, or the arm is circling, tend to

> ## >> **types** of stretching
>
> - **Re-coordination stretches** increase range by changing repetitive motor patterns caused by right or left dominance.
>
> - **Reciprocal stretches** use the natural shortening and lengthening effect on either side of a joint to create more stretch.
>
> - **Fascial stretches** focus on the fascia and help to balance muscle connections; they are particularly effective for opening and stretching the torso.

be re-coordination stretches. They help to break up the body patterns we develop from being right- or left-handed, as well the patterns that come from other reoccurring motions. Merely changing the direction of those familiar patterns can significantly increase our range of motion.

Another stretching strategy has to do with stretching muscles on the opposite side of joints. This is called reciprocal stretching. For instance, when you bend your elbow, the muscles on the front side of the joint—the biceps—shorten, and those on the other side—the triceps—have to lengthen to allow the motion. Using reciprocal stretching techniques automatically relaxes the lengthening side, allowing those muscles to stretch.

Stretching the fascia

Other types of stretches work on stretching the fascia in several ways. Stretching the spine using a breathing and rippling action helps to stretch the torso from horizontal segment to horizontal segment. Another fascial stretch works on stretching the muscle connection chain that runs from the waist, down the back of the leg, and into the foot. This program also includes some stretches specifically designed to glide the arm and leg nerves in their sheaths, which allows greater ease of motion. The details make the difference; read the instructions carefully to find the precision that will give you your best stretch.

The devil's in the detail. Find the precision you need for each stretch by studying the demonstrations and imagining the cues.

>> **muscle** connections

Proper positioning of the arms, legs, and head helps us to physically find the link between muscle and connective tissue. Using focus and intent when we line these extremities up with the torso gives us a powerful tool for changing body posture and developing litheness.

The science of biomechanics identifies various structural body connections and physical forces that are involved in body function. In order to devise appropriate exercises, it is necessary to use our knowledge of the nature of our body parts (how plastic, or changeable, the various components are) to create the effect we need. Three important structural connections in the body that we have to consider are the "X" model, the inner unit, and the lateral system.

The "X" model
The "X" model shows the connection between what is going on externally and the inner unit (see below). It shows how the limbs are connected with each other and how these connections pass right through the inner unit. Think deep; think three-dimensional. The right arm, for example, is connected to the left leg and vice versa. The positioning of the head, which can weigh up to 15 pounds (6.8kg), is also important. Tipping it in any direction activates an intricate system of overlapping muscles that bind the head into the trunk yet allow a marvelous telescoping range to the neck.

The inner unit
Various groups of muscles form the inner unit. These are the muscles at the bottom of the torso (the pelvic floor), the deep abdominal muscles, the transverse abdominals at the sides of the abdomen, the deep low-back muscles, the multifidi (a group

> ## >> **pulling it all** together
>
> - **Coordination** between opposing limbs and the trunk is demonstrated by the "X" model concept.
> - **Precision** in stretching is created by achieving stabilization of the inner unit, which provides a firm foundation.
> - **Elongation of the lateral system** promotes symmetry and balance.

of muscles either side of the spine), and the muscles deep inside the rib cage (the diaphragm).

Working the muscles of the inner unit correctly—with good form—promotes low-back and pelvic health. The exercise instructions also help you to use the inner unit as a stabilizing foundation, giving more precision when you stretch the external parts.

The lateral system
The lateral system connects the muscles and fascia that run down the sides of the body. Think of it as a long road running from the triceps in the upper arm, past the armpit, down the side of the ribs and waist, extending down the side of the leg past the thigh and shin, and ending at the side of the foot. This lateral system is often overlooked, but opening it through stretching is key to balancing the body and improving posture.

The "X" model shows the link between what goes on internally and externally. Opposite sides of the body criss-cross, attaching the limbs and head to the torso.

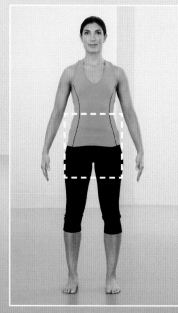

The inner unit is the foundation of our body. It houses our center of gravity. Anchoring this area provides a counterbalance to, and increased effectiveness for, each stretch.

The lateral system extends from the triceps in the arm to the side of the foot.

Attention to stretching the lateral system is a major key in balancing the body. Our right- or left-handed dominance presents a challenge when it comes to achieving optimal posture.

>> **flexibility** and posture

Genetics dictate how flexible you are and also your postural body type. Stiffness and over-flexibility both cause aches, pains, and difficulty in day-to-day activities. Explore your flexibility with these easy tests, and strive to find your best neutral posture.

Gravity has a greater impact upon our posture when we are upright in sitting or standing. If we give in to it, the "segments" of our body collapse (see below left). The result is that our muscles are out of balance and our joints are misaligned.

Stretching counterbalances this and helps you develop a good neutral posture. You start by using good form and working the muscles of the inner unit. This helps you stretch the chest and shorten the upper back muscles, open the low back and engage the abs, as well as stretch the front of the hips and thighs, and the calves.

Practicing sitting and standing tall also solidifies our intent to push vertically upward against the force of gravity. The beauty of this formula is that it applies to all body types and levels of flexibility.

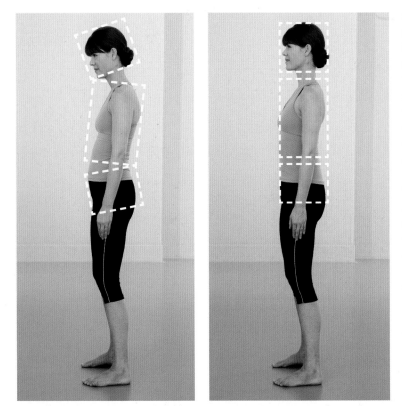

Gravity breaks us into unbalanced segments (far left). The head falls forward. The chest shortens and sinks, and the upper back rounds. The low back tightens and collapses, and the abdomen protrudes. The front of the thighs and hips tighten, while the hip extensors slacken. Body weight lists back on the heels, shortening the calves.

The goal is to balance the segments and achieve neutral posture, with a straight line running from the head through the pelvis (left). Note especially how the weight of the heavy head is now balanced directly over the pelvis, which houses our center of gravity. This alignment puts the least amount of strain on the spine as well as the other joints in the body.

Test the mobility of your shoulders and upper back. Lie on the floor with your arms bent and your forearms parallel with the sides of you head. Your muscles are over-tight if your head and forearms do not touch the floor.

Test the mobility of your spine, rib cage, and neck. From a seated position, cross your arms, put each hand on the opposite shoulder, and rotate your torso. Note how far you can go. Anything less than 35° indicates that your muscles are over-tight. Being right-handed or left-handed affects how far you can rotate.

Test the mobility of your hips. Lie on your back and raise first one leg, then the other. If you can only raise your leg to a 70° angle or less, it indicates over-tightness of your muscles at the back of your leg and hip. Being able to lift each leg to a 90° angle helps prevent low-back pain when sitting. It also prevents walking with an unbalanced gait, which causes leg and back problems. Raising your leg to a 120° angle indicates an exceptional degree of mobility.

>> **imagery** as a tool

Use imagery as a tool to help create precision and a sense of the inner layers of your body in your stretches. Connecting everyday concepts to the exercises gives your stretches an effective edge. Strive to internalize the cues. They hold the key to true physical transformation.

Actors, musicians, and dancers use imagery to help them "act out" their message. Children play imaginary roles in imaginary settings to prepare for adult life. As adults, we can employ imagery to help us make our exercise more effective.

The exercise programs in this book contain some imagery cues that ask you to use your imagination. Focus on them to help coordinate your muscles and access the deeper connections of your body. For example, "Lift the imaginary swimming-pool water" asks you to press upward in the abdomen when you're lying on your front. Mention of "smile lines" is a cue for you to hold your hips in true extension when lying down, and give you the range of motion you need to achieve a neutral pelvis. When you get it right, two arcs separate the buttocks from the upper thighs or hamstrings (see below).

By training these deeper muscles to engage as you perform your stretching exercises, you also train them to engage when you carry out your everyday activities. Although some images apply to certain body positions, such as finding the smile lines while lying on your front, you can also relate to them in other positions. In other words, you can find your smile lines when you're standing, too. They can help you find your neutral posture.

The imagery I use is truly the key to taking your exercise life into your daily life. Study the pictures in the exercises on these two pages, and start a lifelong habit of using your body more completely.

Imagining water pushing up against the abdomen deepens abdominal connections. Visualizing "smile lines" stabilizes the pelvis and brings precision into hip stretches.

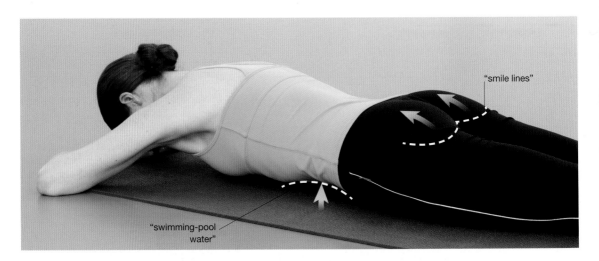

"smile lines"

"swimming-pool water"

Preserve your natural low-back curve by sitting forward on your sitbones. Simultaneously pull the navel to the spine to sandwich the waist with a corset of muscles.

Coordinate the stretch between your head and legs. Reach your head out of the collarbones, like a turtle reaching its head out of a shell. At the same time, balance and reach out through the top foot.

Lift the groin. The floor of the pelvis should be buoyed upward like the air filling a parachute. Feel the lift, like an elevator ascending up the spine toward the head.

15 minute

wake up
the stretch >>

Start to master your stretch
Think three-dimensionally
Focus on body sensations
Breathe smoothly and deeply

>> **wake up** the stretch

Your stretch journey starts with a sequence that creates suppleness and wakes up your stretch. No matter what your level, as you stretch your whole body, you'll find the fluid motion of this sequence as slinky as a long cat yawn. Try to imagine that you're "joining the dots" as you weave your way through each and every movement.

Stretching is a skill that everyone can master. This sequence emphasizes the various techniques you'll need and the sensory elements of stretch that together will help to make your stretch possible. Being able to identify muscle tone is a crucial first step. Next, learning to stabilize one part of the body while another moves away from the stabilizing part is key to the effectiveness of a lengthening stretch. Breathing into tight body areas such as the back of the rib cage demands discipline and focus. Loosening and circling motions help to oil the joints and loosen restrictive connective tissue, thus prompting muscles to expand and contract. Re-coordination exercises make new ranges of motion a possibility for everyone.

The exercises

Feel as much of your body as you can in the Hand pull. Memorize this muscular feeling and strive to carry that feeling into the rest of the sequence. Make the Elbow circles as sensory and luscious as if you were moving through a pool of honey. Direct the flow of your breath very specifically into any tight parts of the diaphragm. This exercise may feel difficult at first, but it can give you a very satisfying sense of relaxation.

The seated exercises may seem easy, but use the surface and structure of the chair to explore your orientation in space. Notice the relationship of your hip, rib, head, arm, and leg placements.

>> **tips for** wake up the stretch

- **Internalize your stretches** by giving as much detailed focus to your body sensations as possible.

- **Try to imagine** the infrastructure—the skeletal part that is moving—such as your arms moving against your upper torso.

- **Work to identify** which parts are anchoring and which parts are moving.

- **Strive to feel the entire path of the motion**, not just the end points.

- **Breathe in long, flowing, time-released breaths**, as suggested by the guide music; be sure not to hold your breath.

The physical boundary of the chair not only provides landmarks so you can judge how far a stretch is moving, it can also give you a sense of your deep muscles, which can help if you feel your movement is restricted. Sitting on a firm surface is also a sneaky way to feel some input up into your sitbones. This pressure gives a neurological stimulus to your "righting" reflex, which helps you to lengthen up against gravity. The Seated cross-leg twist and Shoulder wedge also show you how to press one body part against another to increase the stretch, as well as adding a strengthening element to your stretches.

On the other end of the scale are the Shoulder ovals. They demonstrate an instance where learning to respect a joint's boundary is of great importance, since neck, arms, and shoulders tend to be more sensitive to injury thanks to their potential for extreme movement. The Shoulder ovals also provide a superb nerve stretch and glide—a nerve glide being a movement that creates frictionless motion of the nerve. This, ultimately, will increase the range of movement of the whole of your upper body.

Simple stretching positions while sitting can bring about big changes when you perform them with coordination, precision, and intent.

>> **energizing** hand pull

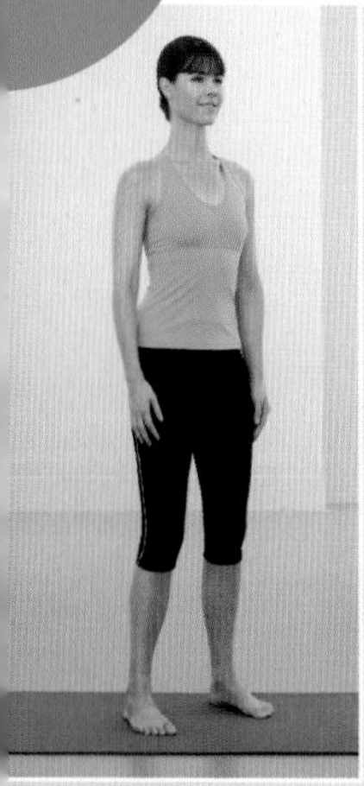

1 **Hand pull** Stand with your hands by your hips, feet just past shoulder-width apart, and toes firmly planted into the floor. Feel as if your legs are pressing outward. Lift your groin muscles toward the head and firm your hips. Slowly exhale as you open your arms to the sides, turning your palms forward.

2 Clasp your hands overhead in an "O" shape, then pull on the hands as if you are trying to pull them apart. Feel as if you are pulling your hands and feet away from each other as you take 2 long breaths. Keep the shape as you exhale and relax for 2 more breaths. Repeat the pull, then relax.

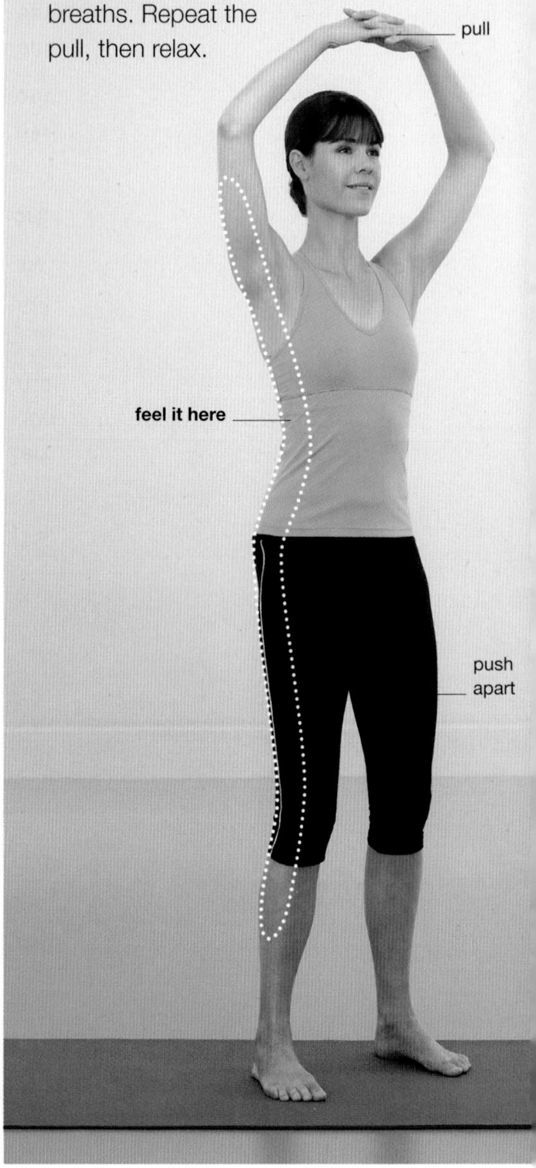

pull

feel it here

push apart

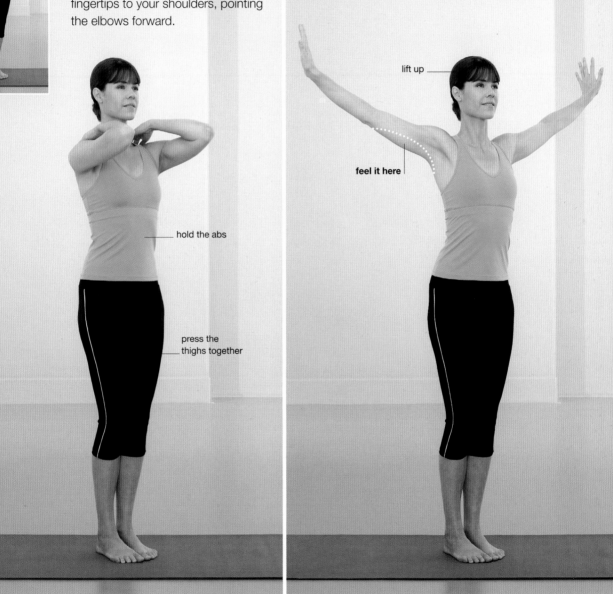

3 **Elbow circles** Bring your feet and inner thighs completely together and place your hands at your hips, with your palms facing forward. Inhale, and fold your elbows to take your fingertips to your shoulders, pointing the elbows forward.

hold the abs

press the thighs together

4 Exhale, lift the elbows, and smoothly circle the hands up and diagonally behind you. Repeat 3 more times.

lift up

feel it here

5 **Rib breath** Keep your legs firmly together as you clasp your hands on the front of your rib cage and try to pinch the crest of the rib cage together. Lift your groin muscles toward the head and stand tall. Then inhale and bring the elbows forward, depressing your chest and breathing into the back of the rib cage.

round the back

6 Reverse the movement. Exhale, open the chest, lengthen up through your head, and look diagonally upward. Allow your elbows to come backward. Repeat 2 more times, inhaling as you bring the elbows forward, and exhaling as you open the chest. Release your hands and shake them gently to release any tension in them.

feel it here

press the ankles together

7 **Side reach** Keep your legs in the same position as you firm your hips and lift your abs up and into the spine. Inhale and reach one arm up and the other down, with palms facing in toward your body.

8 Intensify the stretch by bending the knee slightly on the side of the raised hand and by looking down toward the lower hand. Feel as if someone is pulling your middle finger to the ceiling. Then exhale, straighten the knee, and slowly turn your face forward. Repeat, then change sides and repeat 2 times on the other side. Let your arm come down and relax.

reach up

look down

bend the knee

>> **lengthening** lift & bow

9 **Lift & bow** Sit on the edge of a chair with your feet hip-width apart. Feel your sitbones pressing equally on the seat. Sit tall, lift your groin muscles toward your head, then hold onto one thigh and lift the knee toward the ceiling. Inhale, then lift up into your waist and bow your head toward your knee.

10 Exhale and reverse, lifting your chest and face diagonally up toward the ceiling. Repeat 2 more times, inhaling as you bow, and exhaling as you lift. Lower the foot to the floor and repeat on the other side.

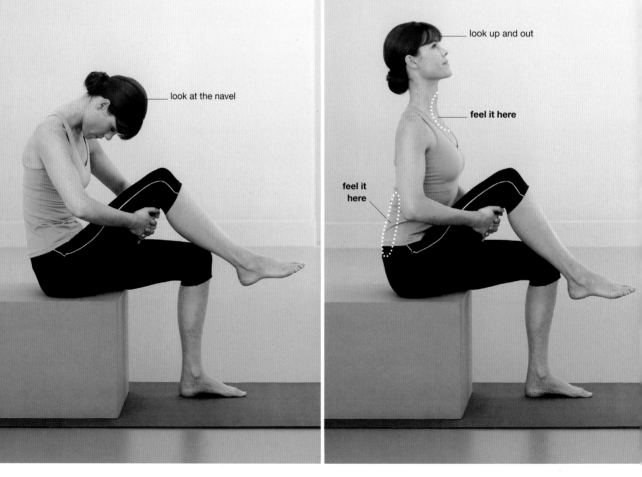

look at the navel

look up and out

feel it here

feel it here

11 **Seated cat** Remain sitting toward the edge of your seat. Extend one foot out on the floor in front of you, keeping the knee a little bent, and pressing the sole and big toe of the foot firmly on the floor. Place your hands on the same thigh. Inhale as you round your back.

12 Exhale and reverse the curve. Start from the lower back, and move through the middle and upper back with a ripple effect to lift the chest and face diagonally toward the ceiling. Inhale, round and repeat, then repeat the whole stretch on the other side. Roll your shoulders and release.

lift the chest

press the toes down

>> **balancing** seated cross-leg twist

13 **Seated cross-leg twist**
Remain seated, cross one foot on top of the opposite thigh, and hold onto your ankle with the other hand. Place the same hand as your crossed leg on your hip. Inhale, lift your groin muscles toward the head, lengthen your spine, and bow your head toward your knee.

14 Exhale, lift your chest, and turn your torso toward your crossed leg. Look past your shoulder. Repeat 2 more times, inhaling as you bow and exhaling as you lift, then repeat 3 times on the other side. Slowly release the leg, come out of the position, and gently move your back to release any tension.

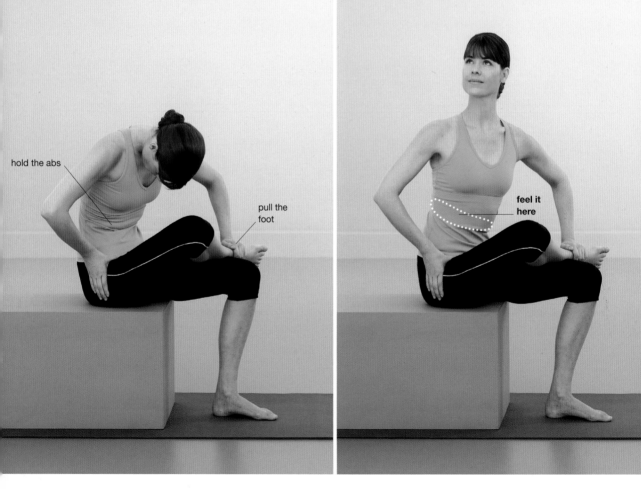

hold the abs

pull the foot

feel it here

15 **Shoulder wedge** Still seated, place your feet shoulder-width apart. Pull your navel to your spine and reach over to the floor. Place one hand on your ankle in between your thighs. Place the other arm outside the leg, then raise that arm as if you were pulling an imaginary thread to the ceiling. Look toward your raised hand.

16 Exhale, keep your arm lifted, and consciously rotate your neck as you look down. Repeat 2 more times, inhaling as you look up, and exhaling as you look down. Bring the arm down and repeat 3 times on the other side. Roll to sit up. Take a deep breath, and relax.

feel it here

feel it here

press the knee against the arm

keep lifting

>> **coordinating** alligator/cat

17 **Alligator/Cat** Go onto your hands and knees. Lengthen your back so it is parallel to the floor, like a table top, then inhale, round your back, tuck your tailbone in, and look toward your navel.

lift the abs

18 Exhale, lengthen your back, then sway your hips and head toward each other. Repeat on the other side, always inhaling as you round your back and exhaling as you take your hips and head toward each other. Repeat 1 more time each side.

sway the hips toward the face

19 **Arm fans** Lie on one side, bend your legs, and lengthen your groin muscles toward your head. Pull your navel to your spine, then reach your arms along the floor, bringing the palms of your hands together in front of your face. Focus your eyes on your top hand as you raise it toward the ceiling, creating a rainbow shape.

eyes follow the hand

20 Continue moving the arm and reach behind you to the floor, allowing your shoulders and torso to rotate with the arm. Try not to move your knees. Exhale, then reach up with the hand as you reverse, "painting the ceiling" with your fingertips until your hands are together again. Repeat 2 more times, inhaling as you open the arm, exhaling as you bring the palms together again. Roll over to the other side and repeat.

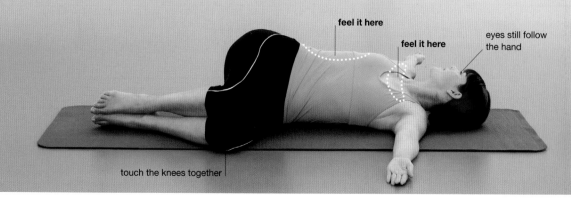

feel it here

feel it here

eyes still follow the hand

touch the knees together

>> **powering** modified cobra

21 **Modified cobra** Go onto your stomach, firm and tighten your hips, and feel the smile lines between your glutes and your hamstrings. Lift the groin muscles toward the head. Feel the imaginary swimming-pool water lifting your abdomen off the floor. Reach your hands out onto the floor in front of you.

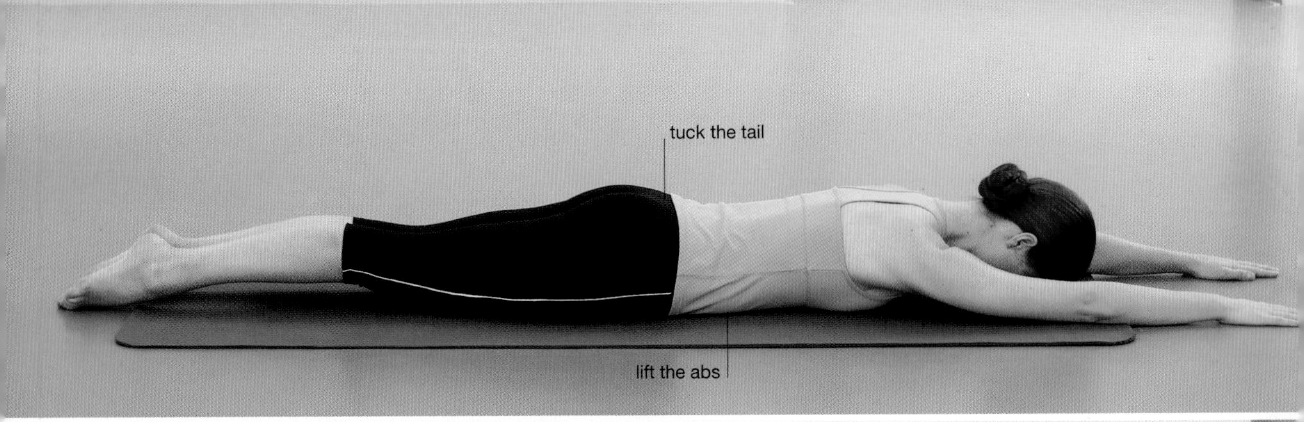

tuck the tail

lift the abs

22 Inhale as you drag your hands along the floor toward your shoulders, keeping the abdomen tight and lifting your front body so your ribs come off the floor. Exhale, slide the arms out in front of you, and take your face back to the floor. Repeat, then relax and breathe normally.

lift the ribs off the mat

23 **Shoulder ovals** Tighten the waist, lift the hips, and come up to a perfect hands and knees position. Point the fingers of the hands in toward each other, then inhale and reach one shoulder down toward the opposite hand.

don't force

point the fingers inward

24 Sweep the chest across the floor, past center toward the other hand, then exhale and continue circling in the same direction as you round your back. Your shoulders should be describing an oval in space. Keep going in the same direction for 2 more ovals, then change direction and reverse for 2 more ovals.

feel it here

make an oval

▲ **Limbering** Elbow circles, page 25   ▲ **Articulating** Rib breath, page 26   ▲ **Articulating** Rib breath, page 26

▲ **Coordinating**
Alligator/Cat,
page 32

▲ **Elongating** Shoulder wedge, page 31   ▲ **Coordinating** Alligator/Cat, page 32

wake up the stretch at a glance

▲ **Energizing** Hand pull, page 24 ▲ **Energizing** Hand pull, page 24 ▲ **Limbering** Elbow circles, page 25

▲ **Balancing** Seated cross-leg twist, page 30 ▲ **Balancing** Seated cross-leg twist, page 30 ▲ **Elongating** Shoulder wedge, page 31

wake up the stretch >>

15 minute **summary**

▲ **Lengthening** Lift & bow, page 28

▲ **Opening** Seated cat, page 29

▲ **Opening** Seated cat, page 29

▲ **Lengthening**
Shoulder ovals,
page 35

cobra, page 34

▲ **Lengthening** Shoulder ovals, page 35

▲ **Coordinating** Side reach, page 27

▲ **Coordinating** Side reach, page 27

▲ **Lengthening** Lift & bow, page 28

Opening
rm fans,
age 33

▲ **Powering**
Modified cobra,
page 34

▲ **Opening** Arm fans, page 33

▲ **Powering** Modi

>> **wake up the stretch** FAQs

The wake up the stretch program is excellent for beginners as well as for someone looking for a lighter, more gentle stretch. During this first program, learn to create focus by coordinating inner and outer muscles through the use of the cues and imagery.

>> ### How is the Hand pull a stretch?

This overhead pull is a sneaky way to stretch the sides of the torso, especially around the armpits, as well as stretching the sides of the hips and legs. Some people will not be able even to reach their hands together in an overhead position, so this exercise makes a great starting point. It's possible that one half of your pelvis is tighter than the other. As you push the legs away from each other, you are beginning to equalize each side, balancing right with left.

>> ### In the Rib breath exercise, it seems as if nothing is moving. What can I do?

You have to have faith that something is happening. The deep connective tissue and the big domelike breathing muscle, the diaphragm, tend to be tight in the back of the rib cage on most people. It's a lot easier to see movement in the front part. Try coughing or sniffing repetitively; feel the action of the diaphragm and ribs in the front. It's anatomically not possible to have a great deal of motion in the back, but in this exercise we begin by cinching the front of the dome, which forces the back to stretch.

>> ### How do I know I'm doing the Side reach correctly?

First be sure you are following the instructions correctly. You have to pull upward very strongly with the armpit, arm, and hand while you bend your knee. It's not going to be a comfortable feeling once you add the turn of the head. The purpose of this exercise is to start opening the rib cage, neck, and shoulders. This is a very dense area and it's hard to tease apart the separate parts.

>> **When I'm sitting, I can barely lift my knee toward my head in Lift & bow, but the model's knee is almost touching. Am I still stretching?**

Absolutely. The important part of this stretch is the lengthening and softening of the spine. I jokingly call this "marinating" the spine. Moving the head up and down also helps to move the spinal cord, which is healthy for the nervous system. Think of it as flossing your nerves. They need to stretch and glide, too.

>> **The model in the Modified cobra is getting way more off of the floor than I am. Does it matter?**

Again, less can be more in this instance, too. Intent goes a long way when we are meeting the boundaries of our limitations. The whole idea is to find out how far you can go in a certain direction. Honor that limitation; don't force it. But meet the boundary, watch the model, and think of the direction of the motion, not so much the endpoint.

>> **The Shoulder ovals are confusing. How do I start?**

This is an extremely effective exercise for the nerves of the arms and neck. Many people don't realize how much restriction they have in their shoulders until they develop a problem. So persist. Start slow. Follow the exact instructions. Sometimes it's helpful to brace your hands on a table and start there first to get the idea of the flow of the movement. Precision is best, but sometimes you just have to gyrate a bit first.

>> **My back doesn't make a round shape like the model's in the Alligator/Cat. What should I do?**

Have faith. Rome wasn't built in a day. Just by attempting the exercise and imagining the shapes you will begin, little by little, to loosen up your back. After just a few weeks, you'll notice your back will feel better and you'll be able to bend and move more easily in everyday life.

15 minute

posture stretch >>

Find your center
Elongate your waist
Extend up against
the force of gravity

>> **posture** stretch

We all desire healthy posture. Although we live in an imperfect world, nearly perfect posture can be achieved by methodically balancing our bodies against gravity's pull. Where the body leads, the mind goes. Improving posture will uplift your outlook on life as well as giving you confidence and endurance against everyday stresses.

Stretching for healthy posture means fighting against the pull of gravity. If we do not work against gravity's pull, then the longer we live, the more bent and deformed we become. A typical gravitational pull creates a forward-jutting chin, a tight chest, and rounded shoulders. Carrying on down the body, the abdomen becomes lax and the low back becomes tighter. A domino effect continues on into the legs, shortening the front of the thighs and creating a loose area around the glutes. The end-result is an off-center line, with tight calves causing the body weight to fall back into the heels. It's no wonder joints wear out before their time. We're all living longer, so our joints—which are a key factor in our quality of life—are important to us. The value of healthy posture cannot be stressed too much. Not only do we achieve a pleasing cosmetic effect by standing upright, we also increase our vitality, since standing well promotes optimal lung capacity, which provides more oxygen for the brain to function well.

The exercises

The Posture stretch sequence follows a muscle-balancing formula as well as reinforcing the neurodevelopmental sequence—in other words, the basic movement patterns that get an infant from lying down to standing and walking. The Posture stretch sequence uses all the positions that infants must achieve on their journey to walking.

> >> **tips for** posture stretch
>
> - **Focus on the ultimate goal** of elongating your entire body in every exercise.
>
> - **Notice how each exercise builds** toward firm, upright posture.
>
> - **Modify when needed**. Be sensible and use extra padding under the knees if they are tender.
>
> - **Enhance balance** by focusing your eyes on a fixed object or by holding onto furniture, if necessary.
>
> - **In the final standing exercise**, focus first on stretching out and elongating your waist as you lengthen your ribs up and off the pelvis; locate your head weight over the center of gravity in the pelvic bowl.

Starting with exercises lying on the back, trunk control is developed which enables optimum control of the limbs. Pay special attention to the various parts of the front of the trunk in the Elongations. Notice how the "W's" exercise straightens and elongates you, combating the typical fetal curling position many adopt when asleep. Next, the Hurdler lat stretch balances both sides of the back of the waist. The Balance point stretch literally pushes the trunk and head up against gravity. Most of us don't notice how our back is pulling us down because our legs compensate, taking up most of the slack in the system. The Sidelying waist stretch stretches the deep muscles we use to stand and walk; be sure to pull the abdomen strongly up and into the spine to get the most benefit from this intense twist.

Progressing to kneeling on both knees usually shows us how tight the front of our thighs and hips can be. The Lunge opener prepares the body for full standing and evens out our walking pattern so that it is not lop-sided. Squatting and then alternating the motion by reaching the hips upward in the Round back squat gives balance and leg strength as well as stretch. The rolling-back motion of the Hanging stretch lets the body register the weight of the trunk and head above the waist. These body parts are heavy, and need to be placed precisely above the firm foundation of the lower body. Ending with a Top-to-toe stretch coalesces the whole body, helping you to stand tall against the ever-present force of gravity.

Kneeling positions help lengthen the front of the body, counteracting hip tightness from prolonged sitting and the slump and fatigue associated with prolonged standing.

>> **centering** elongations

1 **Elongations** Lie on your back, with your legs hip-width apart. Reach your arms beyond your head on the floor and clasp your hands. Inhale and stretch your hands and feet away from each other. Simultaneously press your low back and ribs against the floor.

press the low back down

2 Exhale as you relax, then inhale and stretch again. Finally, exhale and relax one more time.

3 **"W's"** Stay on your back. Reach your arms out to the sides and bend your elbows to 90° with the backs of your hands and forearms toward the floor. If they don't touch the floor, don't force them. Inhale, then press the back of your head, forearms, shoulders, low back, and thighs into the floor.

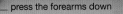
— press the forearms down

4 Exhale and relax, releasing all the tension. Repeat by inhaling and pressing, and exhaling and releasing.

>> **accentuating** "C" stretch

5 **"C" stretch** Still lying on your back, reach your arms up beyond your head on the floor. Take one wrist and, keeping your shoulders against the floor, inhale and pull the wrist toward the opposite side, sliding your upper body slightly along the floor in the same direction.

6 At the same time, cross the leg opposite to the held wrist over the other leg, and slide your legs in the same direction. This adds an extra stretch and helps to make a letter "C" with your body. Stay, inhale, and tense your abdominal muscles, then exhale and lengthen into the "C." Hold for 4 breath cycles. Lengthen and release, move back to center, and repeat on the other side. Thump the thighs to release the low back. Repeat on both sides, then thump the thighs one more time.

keep pulling the wrist

pull the legs

Baby rocks Remain on your back. Exhale, press your back against the floor, and slowly slide your feet toward your hips. Lift your feet, one at a time, and hold onto them from outside your legs, keeping your knees bent. If you can't reach your feet, hold onto your shins.

feel it here

Inhale, pull one knee down toward the floor, and rock toward that side. Then, exhale and release to return to center. Repeat, rocking to the other side, then repeat for 2 more sets.

keep the head on the floor

posture stretch >>

9 **Hurdler lat stretch** Come to a sitting position with both legs comfortably out to the sides. Tuck one foot in toward the groin and reach both hands over toward the extended leg. Sit evenly on your sitbones. Hold wherever it feels comfortable, either at the knee or lower down if you can. Bring both shoulders parallel to the floor. Breathe in, round into your back, and lower your head. Resist the stretch by holding firmly with the hands, on the outside of the leg.

tuck the pelvis under

10 Exhale, pull forward with your hands, round the back even more, and look toward your navel. Repeat 2 more times, then release your hands, roll your shoulders, and repeat on the other side.

feel it here

pull

press the calf down

11 **Balance point stretch** Remain sitting. Bend your knees, slide a hand underneath each thigh, and lift your feet off the floor, finding your point of balance. You will probably need to lean back a little. Use padding underneath your bottom if you need it. Roll your shoulder blades down the back and pull with your arms to hold yourself up. Inhale and bow your head, rounding your back.

feel it here

12 Squeeze your sitbones together and pull down on your arms. Sit tall and lift your groin muscles toward your head. Repeat 5 more times, breathing in as you round, and exhaling as you sit tall.

pull and lift

>> **elongating** sidelying waist stretch

13 **Sidelying waist stretch** Lie on your side with your torso and legs in a straight line, feet pointed. Prop yourself up on your hands, one hand a little behind you. Lift your groin muscles toward your head, and lift your ears toward the ceiling. Inhale, lifting your abs as you rotate the hips forward. Look toward your feet.

hips forward

feel it here

point the feet

14 Exhale. Tighten and firm the hips as you roll them backward. Repeat 2 more times, inhaling as you rotate the hips forward, and exhaling as you roll them back. Turn to the other side and repeat.

hips backward

15 **Front body opener**
Kneel up, with your knees under your pelvis. Use padding underneath your knees if you need it. Tuck your pelvis under and press the hips forward. Find your smile lines. Reach your arms behind you and clasp your hands behind your back, without over-arching the back. Inhale, press your hips together, and squeeze your glutes. Lift your chest and stretch your hands behind you.

16 Exhale, relax your hands, and come back to center. Repeat another 2 times.

feel it here

firm the hips

keep the feet on the floor

feel it here

hold the abs

feel it here

17 **Lunge opener** Come onto your hands and knees. Reach one foot forward, take the other leg back, and lean onto the front leg. Lift the groin muscles toward the head and tuck the pelvis under. Clasp the hands and reach them behind your head, holding onto your skull with the heels of the hands. Inhale, open the elbows, and lift the chest.

18 Exhale. Bring the elbows to point to the front and down. Repeat, then take the other foot forward and repeat.

19 **Round back squat** Come into a squatting position on the balls of your feet. Let your knees open and allow your heels to touch slightly and come off the floor. Bring your hips down toward your heels, then lean more into your hands, place your palms on the floor, and inhale as you lift the hips upward as far as you can. Keep your head down, heels up, and your knees slightly bent.

feel it here

take the feet in a "V"

20 Take a long, slow exhalation as you round your back, tuck your hips in, and lower them toward the heels again, still keeping your head down. Repeat 2 more times.

tuck the tail

allow heels to lift

>> **elongating** hanging stretch

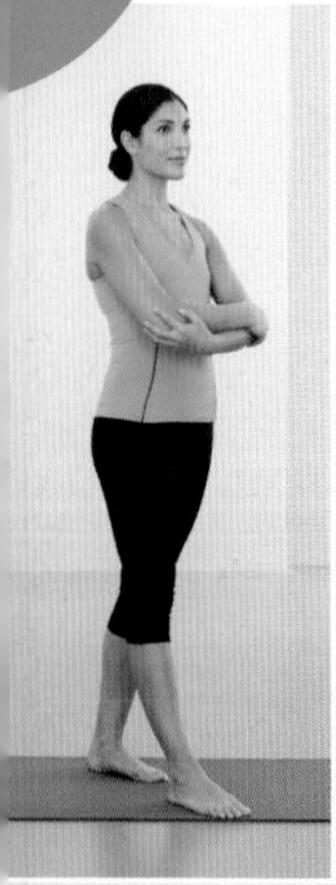

21 **Hanging stretch**
Roll up to standing and place one foot ahead of the other, about your foot's distance and a hand-width apart. Hold onto something if you cannot keep your balance, otherwise fold your arms in front of you and hold onto your elbows. Firm the hips and pull your navel to your spine. Inhale, then tuck your chin under and round your upper back, allowing your head to hang.

22 Exhale, scoop deeper into your spine, and lower your head to hip-height as if you were going over an imaginary fence. Repeat 2 more times, then change legs and repeat on the other side.

take the feet a hand-width apart

keep the tail tucked

stay on the front leg

23 **Top-to-toe stretch**
Roll up to standing. Bring your legs completely together, press the inner thighs together, and lift your groin muscles toward your head. Reach your arms sideways, then take them overhead. Clasp the thumbs and press the palms together. Keep reaching up through your arms, squeezing the head, and pressing down into your feet for 4 breath cycles.

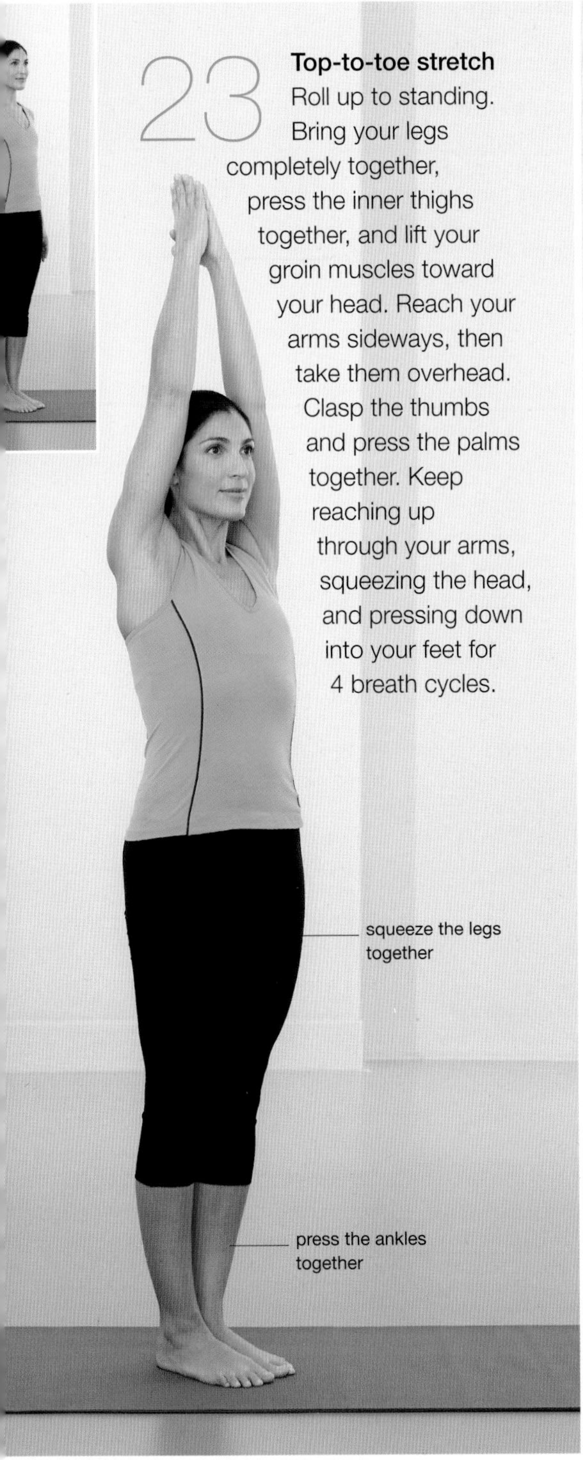

squeeze the legs together

press the ankles together

24 Lower your arms and shake them gently to release the tension. Repeat, then gently move your body to relax any tension.

▲ Accentuating "C" stretch, page 50

▲ Accentuating "C" stretch, page 50

page 49

▲ Opening Front body opener, page 55

▲ Coordinating Lunge opener, page 56

▲ Coordinating Lunge opener, page 56

posture stretch at a glance

Centering Elongations, page 48

▲ **Centering** Elongations, page 48

▲ **Stabilizing** "W's," page 49

▲ **Stabilizing** "W's,"

Elongating Sidelying waist stretch, page 54

▲ **Elongating** Sidelying waist stretch, page 54

▲ **Opening** Front body opener, page 55

posture stretch >>

15 minute **summary**

▲ **Energizing**
Balance point
stretch, page 53

er lat stretch, page 52

▲ **Energizing** Balance point stretch, page 53

▲ **Elongating** Hanging stretch, page 58

▲ **Centering** Top-to-toe stretch, page 59

▲ **Centering** Top-to-toe stretch, pa

7

8

9

▲ **Articulating**
Hurdler lat
stretch, page 52

10

▲ **Softening** Baby rocks, page 51

▲ **Articulating** Hurd

9

20

21

▲ **Limbering** Round back squat, page 57

▲ **Elongating** Hanging stretch, page 58

>> **posture stretch** FAQs

The difference is in the details when it comes to developing and maintaining good posture. Take these tips to heart. Examine yourself in a mirror and learn to see the subtle nuances that cumulatively add up to a vibrant posture. After a while, you're sure to see the changes.

>> What exactly is going on in my body in the Elongations?

Although seemingly simple, the Elongations begin to stretch out every molecule of your body. Think of your body volumetrically, three-dimensionally. Imagine your torso is a cylinder, whose front is much more pliable than the back. Tightening the front helps to stretch out the tighter parts at the back. Elongating the whole body is just like stretching out a long roll of clay, but you have to soften the clay before you can stretch it.

>> My head and arms don't touch the floor in the "W's." What should I do?

Not to worry. Fold a towel and place it under your head. Then place pillows under each arm. It's common for people to start slightly off the floor in the "W's," partly because we rarely lie completely flat in bed at night. I often push away the pillows when I awaken, and then do my "W's" to start the day. It combats the contorted positions we sometimes assume during sleep.

>> The "C" stretch seems hard to do. How can I tell I'm doing it correctly?

Move the upper part of your body first. Then add the lower body. Be sure to feel the entire length of the "C," from the wrist all the way to the ankle. The "C" is so beneficial because it addresses the sides of the body, which are often neglected in more general stretching. Especially when working to achieve postural change, side stretches of the upper rib cage, armpit, waist, and the sides of the legs are necessary to acquire a straighter standing position, and to balance the right side of the body in relation to the left.

>> The Sidelying waist stretch is hard to feel. How can I intensify it?

Make sure you are lifting your groin muscles strongly toward your head. Press your hips forward. The side of the body nearest the floor is again making a long "C" shape. So work to make it as long as possible, reaching your bottom foot away from the ear on the same side. Increase the top curve of the "C" by lifting your uppermost ear toward the ceiling. Use the hands to twist your hips in relation to the shoulders.

>> What do I do if I can't straighten out my hips in the Front body opener?

Don't panic. There's always another way. Kneel on padding if your knees are too sensitive. Usually a mat or folded towel works best. Sometimes pillows are worse because the knees dig into them. Next, squeeze your buttock cheeks together and tighten your glutes, to stretch the front of the hips. Still need help? Balance by holding onto a piece of furniture, press down on your hands, and lift your chest.

>> How do I do the Hanging stretch if my back feels as if it's moving in chunks?

This is a common issue for many people when they start to work with their spine. Think of the spine as being like a child's wooden segmented toy snake. The chunks you feel are groups of those segments moving together, instead of individually. Try to keep thinking about rolling over an imaginary fence and keep imagining the individual parts of the spine moving in turn—the neck, the upper back, the middle back.

>> What must I focus on in kneeling stretches? All I can think about is the pressure on my knees.

First of all, use padding if you feel any discomfort, then you can concentrate on finding your smile lines. Try to press the hips forward and press each knee equally into the floor. This is a great position for gaining low-back strength, and to help to straighten out any leg-length problems.

15 minute

flexibility
stretch >>

Delve into a deeper stretch
Challenge the low back, hips, and legs
Work the hips to open the body fully

>> **flexibility** stretch

Flexibility is best understood as developing your own potential. Each body is unique, with its own set of bone shapes and muscle lengths. Take the challenge here to continue opening your entire body through the gateway of the hips. Hip suppleness is essential to spinal health.

The best way to achieve full body flexibility is to take on the challenge of the low back, hips, and legs. Many people give up when they feel they are not flexible in the hamstrings, but remember that the body also comprises fascial tissue that, among other roles, ties the biomechanics of the upper body to that of the lower body. Now that you've done some loosening and lengthening of your whole body, it's time to focus on a deeper opening of your lower body. This sequence offers more moves that combine stretches with circular, rotational movements. It may require more modification than the first two workouts. Have heart. Challenging yourself with many different exercises will help you to identify your weak areas. There is always a back door to a movement—a way in which you can break it down and simply perform parts of it until they transform into old, familiar friends. Then you can join them together again and you're there!

>> **tips for** flexibility stretch

- **Suspend judgment** about your hip and leg stretch. Slow, steady persistence pays off. Look to yourself, and in yourself, for comparison.

- **Be sure to energize** your upper body as well as your lower body to create the necessary full-body connection.

- **Always use straps**, belts, or bands to modify when needed.

- **Changing the length of tight**, stiff muscles takes time. If your body type is overly flexible, tighten yourself and make the motion or position smaller so as not to over-stretch.

The exercises

The Knee pumps prepare the legs and hips for the next moves. Part of my daily ritual, Knee pumps help to keep my knees and sciatic nerves—the long nerve along the backs of the legs—supple. There is no harm, and it is very beneficial, if you take the extra time to increase the repetitions to as many as 20 on each leg.

The Quad stretch, Thigh sweep, Fouetté stretch, and Figure 4 stretch are absolutely essential to my personal regimen. Go slow at first and take care to observe the transitions from one movement to the next. Work hard to make these transitions smooth; they are actually additional stretches that help to give the sequence its three-dimensional element.

Challenge yourself to master the sequence by imagining you are coaching someone and have to demonstrate and explain each move to them. Being a teacher forces you to think about the nature of each movement and is the best way to clarify them in your own mind.

When you get to Lying hamstring stretch and Advancing frogs, work hard to coordinate all the various parts. It may seem overwhelming to think of them all at once, so first start with the obvious— the basic shape. Again, modify, modify, modify. Rome wasn't built in a day. The next two moves, the Straddle and the Pull-the-thread lunge give you a bit of a rest.

Do try the Angel flight stretch. Remember, your shape and range will be different than our beautiful model's, so start low and slow. This stretch is the ultimate in opening the entire front of the pelvis and thighs. Stick with it, and I promise you will transform beyond all your expectations.

The Cobbler stretch is the gateway to opening the stretch of the hips. In this position, it is important to respect the "voice" of the knees and not over-stretch.

>> **limbering** knee pumps

flex the foot

gently lift the head

1 **Knee pumps** Lie on your back with the soles of your feet on the floor. Lift one foot and hold behind your thigh. Cup and hold the back of your head with the other hand. Inhale as you tuck your chin and slightly lift your head and shoulders. Press your head into your hand. At the same time, straighten the raised knee slightly.

2 Exhale, press your back into the floor, and bend the raised knee at the same time as you lower the foot and head. Repeat, then open the knees slightly to make a "V" shape. Inhale, and repeat the raising and lowering of the head and leg 2 more times. Repeat on the other side.

Baby rolls Still lying on your back, exhale, press your back down, and roll onto one side, bending your knees. Hold your knees, then inhale as you start to roll to the other side, straightening the top knee, then the bottom knee.

press the abs to the floor

feel it here

When you are lying flat on your back, your legs will be open in a brief straddle. Press down on the inner thighs to increase the stretch. Exhale as you bend the top knee and then the bottom knee to roll onto the other side. Continue rolling side to side for 3 sets.

press on the inner thighs

feel it here

5 **Cobbler stretch** Come to a sitting position, take your feet close to the groin, and hold onto your ankles. Sit on a rolled blanket or towel if it helps you to sit up straight. Inhale and lift the shoulders, then slump and round your back, allowing your knees to lift.

6 Exhale and roll your shoulders back and down. Press the knees down toward the floor, as you pull your feet in closer to the groin and lift yourself so you sit taller. Repeat 3 more times.

sit tall

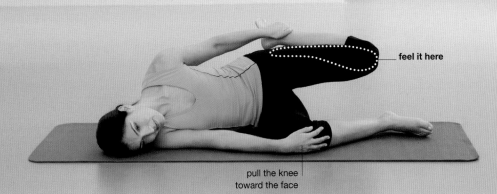

7 **Quad stretch** Lie on your side and bend both knees up toward your chest. Hold onto your bottom knee. Use a pillow under your neck if you feel any strain. Inhale, hold onto your top ankle, and pull your top knee gently toward your chest.

8 Exhale, then smoothly pull your top knee back. Do not let the bottom knee be pulled backward by the top leg. Stay, then pull backward a little more on the top knee. Repeat. Release your ankle and go onto your back, then return to your side and straighten your legs.

feel it here

pull the knee toward the face

>> **elongating** thigh sweep

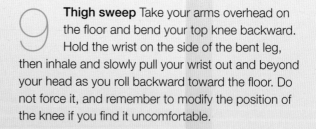

9 **Thigh sweep** Take your arms overhead on the floor and bend your top knee backward. Hold the wrist on the side of the bent leg, then inhale and slowly pull your wrist out and beyond your head as you roll backward toward the floor. Do not force it, and remember to modify the position of the knee if you find it uncomfortable.

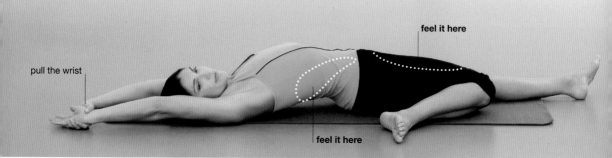

feel it here

pull the wrist

feel it here

10 Exhale, tuck your pelvis under, pull your wrist again, and roll to face forward toward the floor. Repeat, inhaling as you roll backward and exhaling as you roll forward.

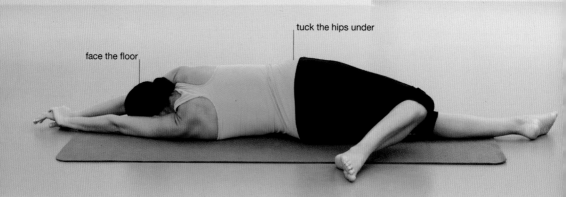

tuck the hips under

face the floor

11 **Fouetté stretch** Still lying on your side, reach your top leg and foot toward the ceiling. Hold onto the calf if you can, or higher up the leg if that is uncomfortable. Lengthen and lift the bottom leg off of the floor. Lift your groin muscles toward your head, lengthen the neck and lift the head. Reach out of the collarbones. Pull your navel to your spine. Tighten your glutes and press your hips forward.

feel it here

reach head away from the foot

feel it here

12 Inhale and slowly roll onto your back. Pull the leg into the hip. Stay and breathe. Repeat one more time.

pull the leg into the hip

press the calf into the floor

13 **Figure 4 stretch** Go onto your back, bend your knees, and place one ankle on the other thigh. Place one hand underneath that thigh and the palm of the other hand on the knee of the crossed leg. Lift the groin muscles toward the head to stabilize the spine. Inhale and pull the hand behind the thigh toward your chest.

pull on the thigh

14 Exhale and press the hand against the knee, away from your face, keeping the bent leg parallel to the floor. If the knee hurts, come out of the position, or loosen the posture. Repeat. Release both legs, thump your thighs, and breathe normally. Roll onto the other side and repeat Steps 7 to 14.

push away

15 **Lying hamstring stretch** Still lying on your back, bend both knees, anchor your pelvis to the floor, lift your groin muscles toward your head, and pull your navel to your spine. Exhale, press your back into the floor, and lift one leg to the ceiling. Take the opposite hand to the lifted leg and hold the outside edge of the lifted foot, or hold lower down the leg if needed. Place the other hand on your thigh, just next to the knee. Inhale and straighten the bottom leg, pressing the calf down to the floor.

16 Exhale and lift the head. Gently press the hand on the thigh away from you. The top foot pulls your leg into the hip socket. Stay for 2 breath cycles, then repeat on the other side. Gently release the legs and thump your thighs against the floor.

pull the foot

feel it here

tuck the chin

press the calf into the floor

17 **Advancing frogs** Come onto your hands and knees, open your knees, reach your arms forward, and squat back, bringing your hips close to your heels. Support your back by lifting the abs. Stay for 2 breath cycles.

lift the elbows

18 Move your torso and arms forward, and come up on your forearms. Actively press the inner edges of your heels into the floor. Your heels will come apart. Lift the groin muscles toward the head to avoid slumping in the low back. Stay for 2 breath cycles.

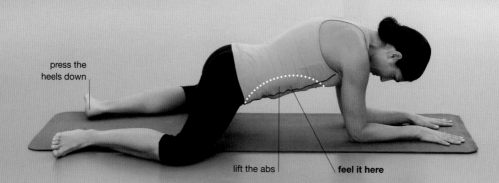

press the
heels down

lift the abs

feel it here

19 Straddle Come to a sitting position, sitting evenly on your sitbones, with your legs open to at least a 90° angle, and with your toes pulled toward your head. Lift your back and open your chest. Sit on a rolled blanket or towel if it helps you to sit up straight, or bend your knees. Lift the groin muscles up toward the head. Open your arms strongly sideways and reach out through the head, legs, and arms.

sit tall

20 Inhale and reach up and over an imaginary fence to one side. Rest the lower hand on the floor behind the outstretched leg. Firm your waist. Exhale, then return to center by "painting the ceiling" with your top arm. Repeat on the other side, then release. Gently roll your shoulders to relax.

reach through the middle finger

pull the navel to the spine

lean on the back hand

press the calves down

>> **stabilizing** pull-the-thread lunge

21 **Pull-the-thread lunge** Go onto your hands and knees, take one leg in front, and lean into it, palms either side of the front foot. Line up the bent-leg knee and toes straight ahead in front of the hip. Press the foot into the floor. Extend the other leg straight behind you and tuck the pelvis under strongly.

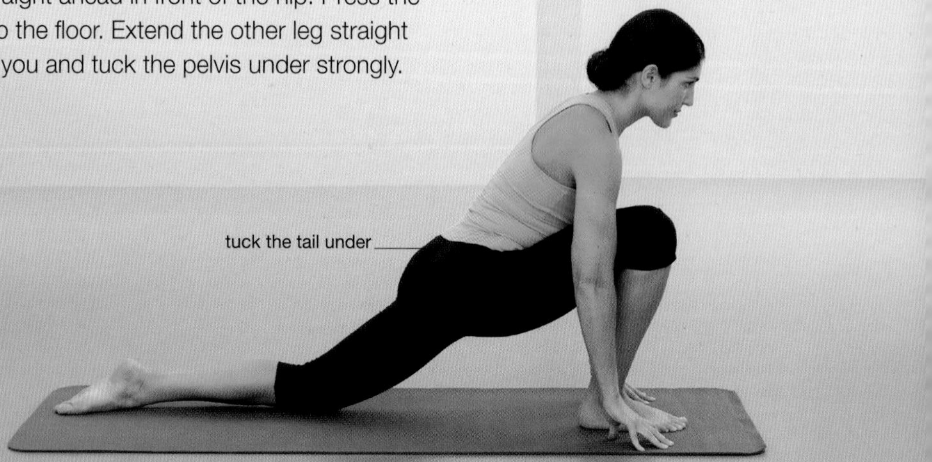

tuck the tail under

22 Pull an imaginary thread up to the ceiling with the hand on the side of the extended leg. Look up at the hand and press down into the floor with the other hand. Stay for 2 breath cycles. Take the hand down to the floor, then repeat with the other leg in front.

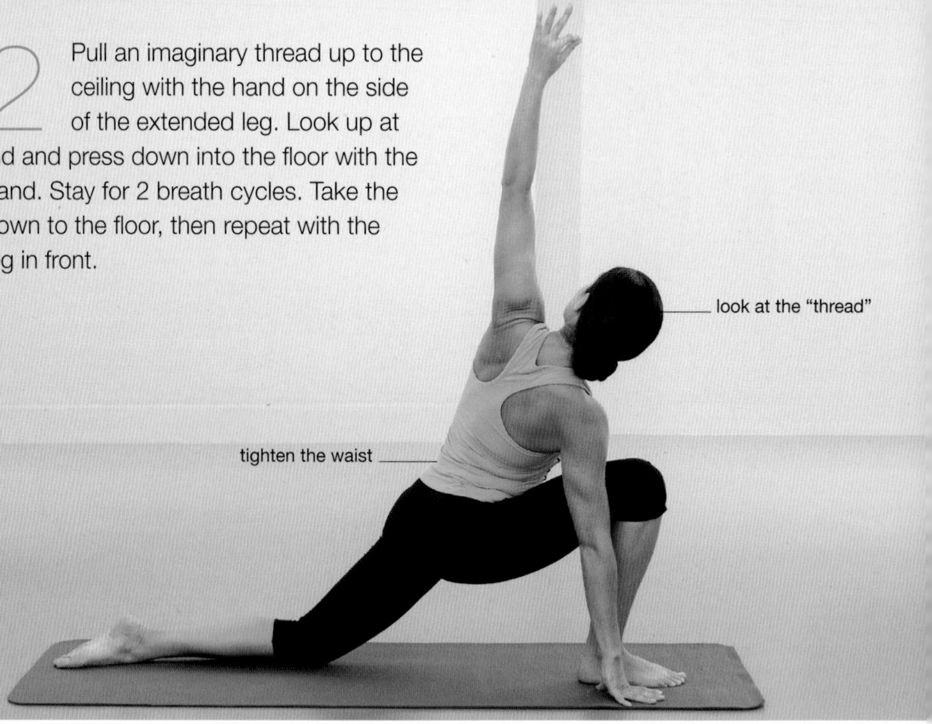

look at the "thread"
tighten the waist

23 **Angel flight stretch** Lie on your stomach, face turned to one side. Feel the imaginary swimming-pool water lifting your abdomen off the floor. Press the tailbone down toward the heels. Inhale, then reach back and bend the knees to hold onto your ankles.

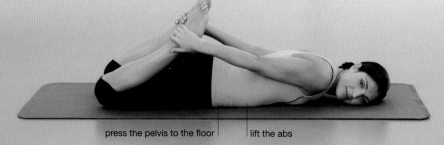

press the pelvis to the floor | lift the abs

24 Exhale, press your feet against your hands, and lift your chest and thighs off the floor to make a bowlike shape. Stay for 2 breath cycles, then release your hands and feet and relax for another 2 breath cycles, breathing deeply.

press the feet
against the hands

▲ **Elongating**
Cobbler stretch,
page 74

olls, page 73

▲ **Elongating** Cobbler stretch, page 74

▲ **Accentuating**
Advancing frogs,
page 80

g hamstring stretch, page 79

▲ **Accentuating** Advancing frogs, page 80

lexibility stretch at a glance

Limbering Knee pumps, page 72

▲ **Energizing** Baby rolls, page 73

▲ **Limbering** Knee pumps, page 72

▲ **Energizing** Baby r

Balancing Figure 4 stretch, page 78

▲ **Coordinating** Lying hamstring stretch, page 79

▲ **Balancing** Figure 4 stretch, page 78

▲ **Coordinating** Lyir

flexibility stretch >>

5 minute **summary**

▲ Stimulating Fouetté stretch, page 77

sweep, page 76

▲ Stimulating Fouetté stretch, page 77

▲ Powering Angel flight stretch, page 83

e-thread lunge, page 82

▲ Powering Angel flight stretch, page 83

Articulating Quad stretch, page 75

▲ Elongating Thigh sweep, page 76

▲ Articulating Quad stretch, page 75

▲ Elongating Thigh

Lengthening Straddle, page 81

▲ Stabilizing Pull-the-thread lunge, page 82

▲ Lengthening Straddle, page 81

▲ Stabilizing Pull-th

>> **flexibility stretch** FAQs

This program begins the true challenge to developing your potential to stretch, so take extra care not to force or strain. Here are some common questions and tips about how to modify positions that seem impossible and how to direct the stretch into the proper location for the best effect.

>> ## What do the Knee pumps stretch?

The Knee pumps stretch many parts of the hips and legs. The inner thigh and hamstring muscles are the most obvious. Not so obvious are the sciatic nerves, the big nerves that run from the pelvis into the legs. Adding the head lifts to the knee movements adds even more stretch. Combining different body parts in one exercise helps to stretch the fascia, the connective bands that hold the body structures together as though they were wrapped in plastic wrap.

>> ## Why do I have to hold onto the bottom knee in the Quad stretch?

Holding the bottom knee ensures that the stretch is being directed into the front of the hip joint and not into the waist line. It may seem awkward at first, but with time it will become natural. Work hard to find the line between the buttocks and the hamstrings as you pull the foot backward. This will help you to gain the best possible stretch of the front of the dense thigh.

>> ## What do I do if my knee hurts in the Thigh sweep?

Always make sure your knee is not over-stretching in any of the stretches. You should never feel pain directly in the knee. If it does hurt, you can simply straighten the leg on top, open your legs slightly, and brace them against the floor. Then, tighten your hips and press them forward as you pull on the wrist, turning the chest forward and back.

>> What does "fouetté" mean, and what does this exercise achieve?

It means "whipped" and the action is easy to see when a ballet dancer performs a fouetté. The movement gives a three-dimensional stretch deep inside your hip. You have to imagine the internal roundness of the hip joint, the way the head of the thigh bone moves in the socket of the pelvis. The circular movement created by the Fouetté stretch improves the mobility of that joint and of your entire pelvis.

>> Is it necessary for me to hold the outside of the opposite foot in the Lying hamstring stretch? I can't reach it.

This is an instance where having a stretching strap can come in handy. A bath robe belt also works well. Loop the belt around your foot and hold it with the hand on the opposite side. Do press the other hand against the thigh of the lifted leg, even if you cannot straighten the leg. You have to start somewhere. You can and will improve.

>> I can't even remotely begin to get into the Angel flight stretch. Can you help?

This is a challenging exercise, even for veteran stretchers. Again, the use of a belt can help here. You can even start by holding one leg, then the other since there are two repetitions of the exercise. An alternative is to lie on your stomach on the floor with your feet behind you over a sofa seat. Then press your hands against the floor and lift your chest as in the Modified cobra.

>> I only feel pressure in my knees in Advancing frogs. Where should I feel the stretch?

First, try to get your knees as open as possible and place the weight on the inside of the knees, not on top of the kneecaps. You should feel the stretch deep in the innermost fold of the leg at the groin. Be sure to keep the waist lifted since that takes pressure off the inner thigh. Use your hands and forearms to direct the pressure back and down toward the inner thigh.

15 minute

strength stretch >>

Find your peak of performance
Be strong yet lithe
Fluidity leads to ease and grace

>> **strength** stretch

You don't need to be a contortionist to master this final sequence. Use your body control to guide you into these more advanced movements. Regard it as your ultimate goal. Even beginners can discover how much control they need to exert, whether they are trying to balance in a precarious pose or performing the simplest stretch.

Strength by definition means grounding and control. See this sequence as one feat of strength after another in an Olympic trial. Close up, one can see the suppleness of the athlete's body, and in action you can see the litheness of their motions. Think of all the hours of preparation Olympic athletes must endure to reach their final goal. In this sequence, look at each exercise as a goal in and of itself. The trick is to break each exercise down by starting small and gradually building to a larger and steadier range of motion. Remember that achieving a general level of fitness takes about two months of practice, and developing a split may take more like six months, depending on how naturally flexible you are. The recipe for Olympic development is to stress the body, then to rest it. Be smart and give your body a good rest after practicing this sequence. The poses and movements here move toward a crescendo that primes you for success.

The exercises

Set the tone for strength by standing tall in the Butterfly stretch and the Upper side bend. Feel your upper body moving against the lower body, as if your lower body were rooted and anchored, like a great oak tree. The series of squats that follows coordinates the strength and suppleness of the spine with the suppleness of the legs. Get more benefit by opening your knees as wide as

> ## >> **tips for** strength stretch
>
> - **Think of your spine** and legs grounded like the trunk and roots of a great oak tree.
>
> - **Remember, you're not failing** if you need to use props and smaller positions to start to get familiar with the exercises.
>
> - **Find your "pelvic diaphragm,"** and keep looking for ways to coordinate your inner muscle strength as you work with larger movements.
>
> - **Always be careful** with large stretches of the neck. Never pull on the head.

you can in the Wide squat twist and in the Deep squat. These squats also provide a great opportunity to strengthen the "pelvic diaphragm"—the parachutelike muscle layer that lies at the bottom of the torso.

As you perform the next exercise, the Neck stretch, be mindful that you are now coordinating the "neck diaphragm"—the parachutelike muscle and soft tissue layers defining the top of the rib cage—with the pelvic diaphragm. So this sequence works on more than meets the eye. It is the ultimate in strength and control. Become willing acquire the ability to coordinate deep muscles with the larger, more obvious muscles, such as the abs, the glutes, and the thighs.

Continue this coordination as you now ripple the spine more strongly in the Kneeling cat and the Kneeling side stretch. The goal is not whether you can approximate the position, but whether you can make such a rangy pose and still coordinate the deeper muscles. Keep this concept activated in the Fish stretch. The last three exercises are the most challenging of all. I have faith in you, and know that little steps make big leaps possible. Modify. Go slowly. Every attempt warrants a gold star of success. Keep your eyes on the prize; the application of stretch with control. Fulfill the potential of your body, one step at a time.

Connecting the deeper core muscles while tensing the larger, outer muscles in these strength stretches adds value and effectiveness to your work.

>> **limbering** butterfly stretch

1 **Butterfly stretch** Stand with legs completely together and pressing the base of the big and little toes, and the middle of the heel of both feet on the floor. Lift your groin muscles toward the head. Pull your navel to your spine. Clasp your hands behind your head, inhale, and lift up and forward from your waist. Simultaneously bow your head, bend your knees, and bring the elbows toward each other.

2 Exhale, straighten the legs, and stretch up and out of your waist, fanning the elbows open. Reach out through the points of the elbows and feel as if your breastbone is being pulled up toward the ceiling. Repeat, then relax and shake the hands.

feel it here

feel it here

anchor the feet

Upper side bend Still with your legs completely together, renew your ⟩rm. Lift the groin muscles ⟩ward the head, and pull the ⟩bs up and into your spine. Clasp ⟩ur hands behind your head.

Inhale and lift up and out of the rib cage, over an imaginary fence under one armpit. Tilt one elbow down toward the floor, the other up toward the ceiling. Exhale and take your shoulders back to center. Feel a "V" of strength from the small of the low back to the points of the elbows. Repeat on the other side, and then repeat one more set.

tighten the abs

lift over the "fence"

anchor the feet

>> **lengthening** flat back squat

5 **Flat back squat** Lift the abs and roll down your spine into a squatting position. Let your knees open and go onto the balls of your feet. Lean on your hands, then inhale as you lift diagonally up and out with your chest, keeping your back flat and extended. Imagine you are looking under a table.

6 Exhale slowly as you lift the hips upward, taking the heels as high as you can. Straighten your knees and tuck your chin into the legs. Keep lifting the groin muscles toward the head. Stay and breathe, then repeat, intensifying the stretch at the end. Lower and relax. Repeat.

feel it here

tuck the toward t▶

lift heels high and mind your balance!

7 **Wide squat twist** Come to a standing position with your feet wider than hip-width apart and your toes facing outward. Lift the groin muscles toward the head, inhale, and lower your hips. Bring your hands to the thighs, take some of your weight into them, and check that your toes are in line with your knees.

8 Inhale, then press backward on one hand on the inside of the knee, twisting that shoulder down. Look up and out in the opposite direction. Stay for 2 breath cycles, then exhale and bring the shoulders back to center. Come up, shake your legs a little, and repeat on the other side.

toes open out

feel it here

press back on the knee

>> **sustaining** deep squat

9 **Deep squat** Resume the wide position of the legs, with your feet wider than hip-width apart and your toes facing outward. Inhale, lift the groin muscles toward the head, and slowly lower your hips. Hold onto your ankles or hold higher up the legs if that is more comfortable.

10 Keep lifting the groin muscles, then press your elbows back against the inner thighs. Stay, then slowly come up, gently shake your hands and legs, and relax.

press the elbows backward

hold the ankles firmly

feel it here

sit on the hand,
palm upward

11 **Neck stretch** Find a comfortable sitting position on the floor, preferably with legs crossed. Sit on a rolled blanket or towel if it helps you to sit up straight. Place one hand, palm up, underneath the sitting bone. Drape the other arm over the head to reach the ear. Breathe into the area between the ear and the tip of the shoulder. Inhale, then tilt the chin diagonally down.

12 Gently turn the head diagonally upward and lift the eye focus. Breathe into the new area of tightness in your neck to release it. Carefully turn the face forward, undrape your arm, rub your neck, and gently roll your shoulders. Repeat on the other side.

>> **elongating** kneeling cat

feel it here

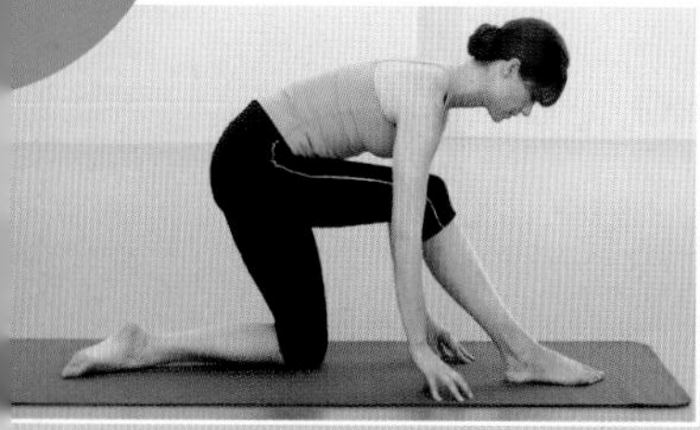

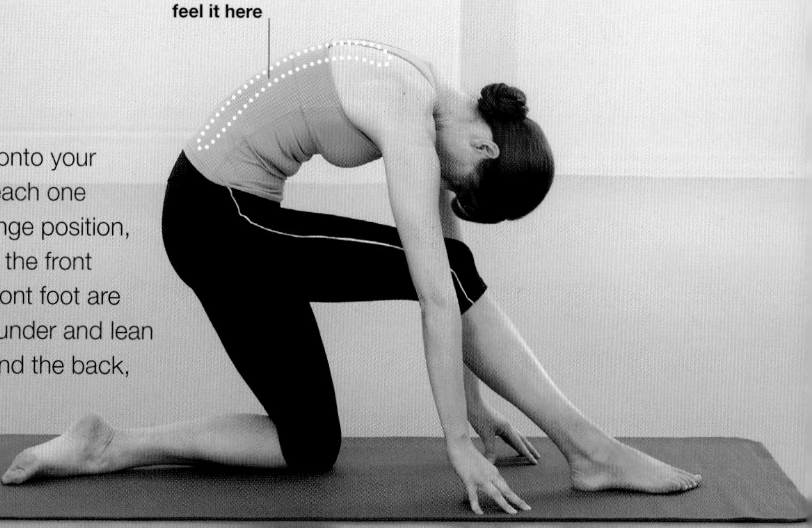

13 **Kneeling cat** Come onto your hands and knees. Reach one foot forward into a lunge position, hands on the floor either side of the front leg. Make sure the toes of the front foot are flat on the floor. Tuck the pelvis under and lean toward the back leg. Inhale, round the back, and look at the navel.

14 Open your mouth, exhale from the back of the throat, lengthen your low back, then start arching your back and lifting your chest. Imagine you are looking under a table. Repeat, inhaling and rounding, and exhaling and arching. Repeat on the other side.

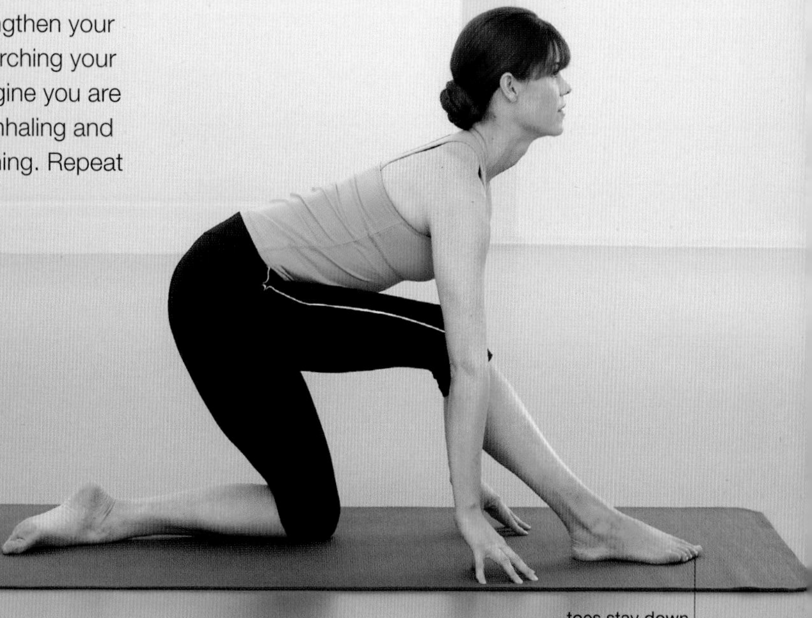

toes stay down

15 **Kneeling side stretch**
Starting on your hands and knees, take one leg diagonally in front, knee bent, sole of the foot on the floor. Turn both legs out slightly, lower the head, and take the arms in front of you, touching your middle fingers together. Then roll up through the spine and fan your arms open sideways.

16 Tuck your pelvis under and reach your top arm up and over toward the bent leg. Rest your lower forearm on the thigh of the bent leg. Reach up and out through the third finger of the top arm. Lift the groin muscles toward the head. Stay for 3 breath cycles, then repeat on the other side.

feel it here

feel it here

feel it here

17 **Fish stretch** Lie on your back, knees bent, soles of the feet on the floor. Place your palms on the floor by your hips. Exhale, then gently press the low back forward and arch your back slightly.

arch the lower back

18 Roll your shoulder blades back and down, then press down on your forearms and arch your back more to come up onto the top of your head. Put as little pressure on the head as possible. Stay for 1 long breath cycle. Relax, then repeat.

minimal pressure on the head

19 **Thigh lunge** Go onto your hands and knees. Lengthen your back so it is parallel to the floor, like a table top. Reach one foot forward into a lunge position and take your hands to the floor either side of the foot.

feel it here

20 Tuck the toes of the back foot under, lengthen the leg back behind you, and straighten the back knee. Lift the groin muscles toward the head and, balancing, place one hand and then the other on the front thigh. Press the hands down on the thigh and lift the chest. Stay for breath cycles. Exhale and release, then repeat on the other side.

firm the hips

stand on the toes

21 **Pigeon arabesque** Sit with one leg bent back and the other bent forward. Your legs should make the letter "Z" with your back knee touching the front foot. Place your hands on the floor in front of you. Straighten the back leg behind you, with the knee pointing toward the floor. Lift your groin muscles toward your head.

tuck the tail under

balance on the thigh

22 Hold your position and reach the arm on the same side as the back leg out in front of you. Reach the arm on the bent leg side out to the side. Stretch up through the head. Stay for 2 breath cycles. Switch legs and repeat.

23 **The split** Switch legs and resume the "Z" sit, then lengthen the back leg behind you. Lift your groin muscles toward your head and pull your navel to your spine. Lean on your hands.

use the hands if necessary

24 Switch legs, resume the "Z" sit, lengthen the back leg behind you, and renew your form. Find your balance, reach your hands behind you, clasp them, and try to straighten your elbows. If you prefer, you can stay with hands at your sides for balance. Stay for 2 breath cycles, then release. Come onto your back and thump your thighs.

tighten the abs

feel it here

feel it here

▲ **Opening** Upper side bend, page 97　　　▲ **Lengthening** Flat back squat, page 98　　　▲ **Lengthening** Flat back squat,

▲ **Balancing** Kneeling side stretch, page 103

▲ **Centering**
Fish stretch,
page 104

▲ **Centering** Fish stretch, page 104

mbering Butterfly stretch, age 96

▲ **Limbering** Butterfly stretch, page 96

▲ **Opening** Upper side bend, page 97

Elongating Kneeling cat, page 102

▲ **Elongating** Kneeling cat, page 102

▲ **Balancing** Kneeling side stretch, page 103

strength stretch >>

5 minute **summary**

10

▲ **Sustaining** Deep squat, page 100

▲ **Articulating**
Neck stretch,
page 101

▲ **Articulating** Neck stretch, page 101

▲ **Coordinating** Pigeon arabesque,
page 106

▲ **Energizing**
The split,
page 107

▲ **Energizing** The split, page 107

▲ **Stimulating** Wide squat twist, page 99

timulating Wide squat twist,
age 99

▲ **Stimulating** Wide squat twist, page 99

▲ **Sustaining** Deep squat, page 100

owering Thigh lunge, page 105

▲ **Coordinating**
Pigeon
arabesque,
page 106

▲ **Powering** Thigh lunge, page 105

>> **strength stretch** FAQs

Honesty and attention to detail are what make all the difference when it comes to bringing true strength to your stretch. Physical development takes time, so be patient. Here are some common questions and answers to help you in your quest to find your true physical potential.

>> **I get dizzy during the Flat back squat. Is there anything I can do to prevent the dizziness?**

Dizziness is common when people first start doing upside-down exercises. The inner ear may not be used to inverting the head, and this is why you may feel some dizziness. But it's healthy to move the head in different orientations in an active movement for a limited time. The eyes usually control most of our balance. Simply keeping your eyes open, and going slowly will help your body to accommodate to the position.

>> **What if my hips don't go down very far in the Wide squat twist and the Deep squat?**

Just go down as far as you feel you can support the position. You'll still get a great groin stretch. Another option would be to hold onto a chair or other piece of furniture to steady yourself. Then you might find that you are able to bend more deeply into the squats. Consistent practice definitely makes for improvement in this stretch.

>> **My head doesn't bend well to the side for the Neck stretch. Should I pull harder?**

First of all, never pull on the head; let gravity and the simple weight of the arm do the work. Over time it will open up. This is an exercise that truly requires precision and care in its execution. It gives a fabulous stretch of the different muscles of the neck. To access all those muscles, be sure to keep the head bent to the side, however slightly, as you turn your face.

>> I'm not feeling much stretch in the Kneeling cat. How can I find the stretch?

A common mistake here is to let the weight of the hip move toward the front leg. Be sure to keep the hips moving backward, especially as you lift the chest upward. Another tip is to literally stick your buttocks back and up, trying to arch the low back as you lift your chest. Yet another tip is to keep your chest as low as possible to the leg throughout the exercise.

>> I feel as if I'm not going anywhere in the Fish stretch. Is there some trick to it?

Some people's body types mean they are able to arch their low back better than other people. It's purely structural. Don't ever force a position. If you can't get the stretch in this area, try propping a firm pillow or ball in between your shoulder blades. Practice by placing it there, bracing yourself onto your forearms, and squeezing between the shoulder blades for several breaths.

>> Is going into The split necessary to consider myself really flexible?

Not really. As with the Fish stretch, body type often determines how naturally flexible you are. The main goal is a comfortable, pain-free body. Sometimes flexibility is undesirable, especially if a person's level of strength is too low to sustain the increased range of motion. A lithe body is preferable to a loose, disorganized body. That's why it's so important to emphasize the strength aspect as you develop your stretch.

>> How can there be both stretch and strength in one exercise?

Strength is found in stretches by tensing the muscles in noncollapsed positions. Inversions and bending the spine over closed legs use your body weight as resistance to aid strengthening. Different bodily orientations, and moving hard-to-reach areas such as the rib cage create comprehensive strength. Strengthening many small parts leads to greater strength overall.

15 minute

moving on >>

Life propels us into forward
motion and change
Incorporate stretching for
a healthy life

>> **modify** as needed

It's not a failing to change an exercise to suit your needs, whether it's because of pain, age, or stiffness. There's a back door to every stretch. Nor is it cheating to use props and modifications. It's just plain wise.

The body can move in multiple directions with a great deal of ease, yet people are often deterred from doing stretching exercises because they worry about feeling discouraged. We would all love to look like the models featured in this book, but use them to help you see the stretching exercises clearly, not to compare yourself with them.

Some of the stretches may feel a little strange or unusual, especially if you are new to exercise. Part of the reason we stretch in unusual positions is to identify our weak links, so pay attention and focus on what feels too tight, too loose, or painful.

If an exercise doesn't feel right, there's always a way to make it more accessible. Some people hav trouble sitting on the floor because they have tight hamstrings, glutes, or tightness in the low back, o a combination of one or more of these. Sitting on a foot stool, ottoman, towel, or bolster can give just the lift needed to make the stretch possible.

Knees should never hurt during stretching. If they feel painful, support them on pillows or bolsters to take the pressure off. Another tip for this pose is to move the feet farther away from the groin.

ay special attention to your knees and monitor hem for signs of pain or discomfort. "No pain, no ain" definitely does not apply to these complex bints. If you need to, prop them up with pillows when you are sitting to take the strain off the gaments. If they feel tender when you kneel on hem in weight-bearing positions, support them with some form of padding. Straighten them out f a bent-leg position if it's uncomfortable. If one f the knees refuses to straighten, as it might in he Lying hamstring stretch, use a towel, belt, or trap to reach the foot.

You can increase or decrease the intensity of a stretch as it suits you (perhaps your body feels different on different days or at different times of day) by pulling or extending more or less. Breathing and relaxing help you stretch farther. Alternatively, try modulating the intensity of a stretch by elongating in a progression from one to ten, and then reducing it. The level of intensity should never go into the "strain zone" and you should not have extreme pain after you have performed your stretches. Remember: compare only yourself to yourself to make the greatest gain.

Help for different stretches. A towel over the toes acts as a strap for a hamstring stretch—elastic exercise bands don't work as well. A book under the pelvis (right, above) will help you to sit forward on the sitbones. A rolled towel placed under the head straightens the neck and helps you avoid neck pain (right, center). A towel is excellent as padding when you are kneeling (right, below).

>> **stretches for** everyday life

It's easy to take your stretches into everyday life. Notice how you move when you are grooming, dressing, even cooking and cleaning, and turn each movement into a stretch. And think "office" as well as "home" to get the most out of your stretch regime.

Look at the ways your body moves in everyday life. Notice how different movements feel, such as brushing your hair or pulling on a sweater or pants. Does the task feel comfortable? Do you have the same range of motion from one side to another? How does it feel to bend over to reach to a pet? Let your answers to these questions guide you to set yourself goals that will make an action a little easier or smoother.

Gradual changes

Changes to the way we move happen gradually over time. Diminishing range of motion creeps up on people of every age. A student notices writing arm and shoulders tightening during a long exam. A young mother notices a tight chest or sore low back as she holds or reaches down to a toddler. Older adults notice they can't bend to the floor or reach up into cupboards as easily as in times past.

Your adaptable body

Life's distractions, such as being preoccupied with a demanding job, with a new baby, or with having to juggle a long commute with household duties can sideline us from regular physical activity. Then suddenly we notice a change and start to worry that our bodies are not as mobile as they once were.

The good news is that your body is adaptable. It changes to accept what the environment is telling it to do. If you inadvertently restrict its motions—for instance, by sitting for long periods—it adapts to the smaller, less frequent motions. Conversely, it can re-adapt. That's why it's important to find ways in everyday life to get an extra little bit of stretch. Small changes can keep your body healthy over time.

In a crowded schedule

It's commendable to devote an hour or two a day to getting exercise, but not everyone can do that. Our 15-minute programs make it possible to get exercise, even with the most crowded schedule. Yet neither should you overlook the power of taking 25 seconds—four breath cycles—to feel the stretch in an everyday position or movement. This will add to your overall physical wellbeing. Using this strategy during those overwhelming times of life, when every second appears to be accountable, will pay off handsomely.

Brushing your hair is a great way to stretch the shoulders and chest. Try switching the brush to your nondominant hand to balance each side of the body.

Putting on your socks is a good time for a hamstring stretch. Simply lift the leg, or reach over to it, bow the head, and take a few breaths.

Working in an office gives you a good opportunity to use some chair stretches from the Wake Up The Stretch program. Reach your hands behind your head and wing your elbows open in a chest stretch. It helps your workday go faster and more smoothly. Sitting work is probably some of the most tiring, and it's important to take frequent breaks, even for a few breaths. Office stretches increase clear thinking as well as helping to avoid computer overuse problems that can affect your chest, hands, and arms. Intermittent breathing and stretches will make you a more productive worker, whatever you do for a living.

An everyday habit

Perseverance is simple when you make stretches an everyday habit. Habits can be formed in as little as 21 days, so set a goal on your calendar for the next 21 days and find opportunities for a stretch at home, work, and play. Have faith: the body will change, but only with persistence. Stretching in everyday life makes that persistence easy.

Take a twist break at the office. Cross one leg over the other and turn in the direction of the crossed leg, just as in our Seated cross-leg twist.

>> **everyday stretches** that make a difference

- **Reach a little farther** to stretch into that cupboard. Take a break. Yawn to stretch the jaw. Open the eyes and look upward to open the chest and neck.

- **Stretch your legs and hips** when putting on and taking off clothes. Practice lunges when vacuuming and move your hips from side to side when sweeping.

- **Renew your posture at the office** by squeezing between the shoulder blades and rolling your shoulders. Firm the glutes and sit up tall.

>> **relaxation** techniques

Relaxation takes discipline in a busy world. Chores, obligations, and crises sap energy reserves and present road blocks to emotional balance. Try these scheduled and unscheduled calming techniques to make relaxation a priority in your life.

Relaxation is great for renewing the body, mind, and spirit. During every waking hour we expend our physical and mental energy, so we need to replenish it. Take a cue from professional athletes who aim for peak fitness. They know that the key to achieving optimal functioning lies in alternating periods of stress with times of relief and rest.

We all need a certain amount of stress in our lives to challenge and motivate us. But we also need to shake off any fatigue on a regular basis to avoid chronic weariness.

Sleep and rest

It's important for us all to renew our resources with nightly sleep and timely rest. Developing a healthy nightly ritual is essential in establishing an optimal renewal plan. Make your bedroom a sanctuary by creating a soothing, quiet place with your favorite

Use the contract–release method to lessen the tensions in your body. One by one, tighten and release each body part. End by tensing your whole body (inset, below), then let go and breathe deeply (main picture, below).

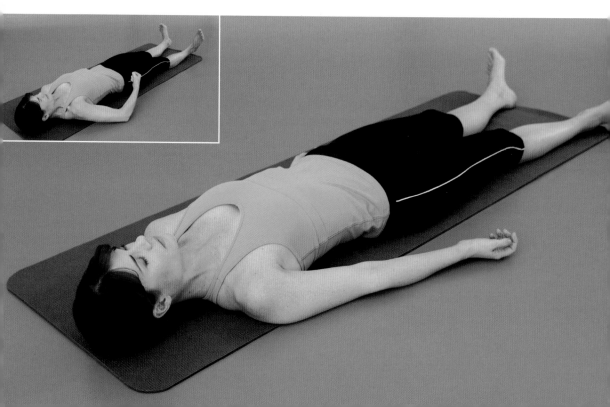

>> **tips for** dealing with daily stress

- **To cope with life's ups and downs** be sure to make time daily for refreshment and restoration.

- **Manage your stress**. Try a progressive relaxation technique, breathe deeply, or learn to meditate to reverse the effects of stress.

- **Develop good sleep hygiene**. Make your bedroom an inviting, quiet, peaceful sanctuary and let go of the day's hassles and worries.

Practice deep breathing. The diaphragmatic breath is found by placing your fingers at the bottom of your breast bone and sniffing or coughing a few times. Inhale deeply; feel the rib cage expand.

bedding and gentle lighting. Don't have the television or your computer in the bedroom. It should be a space strictly for unwinding.

Don't drink alcohol last thing at night. Instead, savor a cup of a caffeine-free drink for an uninterrupted night's slumber. Some people find a warm bath before bed helps to relax them. Light reading material can also quiet the mind and help you leave the day's worries behind you. Make sure the room is completely dark while you're asleep. Studies have shown that exposure to light during sleep can disturb your body's natural cycles.

If you awaken during the night, focus on the pleasant texture of the bedding, take deep breaths, and relish the luxurious time you have for rest. Strive to get seven to eight hours of the deep sleep you need for complete physical restoration.

Using stretching to help you relax

Relaxation techniques can greatly influence the restoration cycle. Simple exercises such as the progressive contract–relax technique (see opposite) can quickly lower body tension and take your mind away from overly analytical thoughts. For instance, tense the fists as you count to ten, then relax them. In order of progression, apply the same tense-then-relax method to the shoulders, thighs, calves, feet,

abdomen, and finally the face, puckering your lips and eyes strongly. End the technique by tensing your entire body, and then completely let go of all your body tension as you breathe five deep, long breaths. Notice how relaxed your body and your mind have become.

Another simple yet reliable relaxation technique, excellent for any setting and any location, is deep diaphragmatic breathing (see above). Place your fingers at the bottom of your breast bone to find the way your diaphragm moves. Sniff quickly several times or cough to feel the muscles move. Breathe into the diaphragm and feel these muscles expand for four seconds (think "1-alligator, 2-alligator", etc.). Then exhale for 8 seconds. Slow breathing reverses the fight-or-flight, adrenalin-based panic that's part of our fast-paced society.

>> **strategies** for healthy living

We all strive to achieve a good quality of life, whether we're just starting out or have reached retirement. Work, play, good nutrition, and the ability to relish the joys and cope with the disappointments of life are all a part of the equation that will bring us health and contentment.

Wouldn't you rather live in a high-functioning, optimal way than a low-functioning one? Physically, we need energy to meet the demands of the day. We want to move around and lift and bend without pain or limitation, which is where the stretching programs in this book come into play. Mentally, we want to be alert and keep our homes and jobs running well. Emotionally, it is preferable to be stable, acting instead of reacting, in our family and professional encounters.

Balance and positivity

There are many things in life that we cannot control, so focus on those you can. A good starting point is a healthy, well-balanced diet. Eat five servings of fruits and vegetables and about three 3-ounce servings of protein (meat, fish, dairy, eggs, grains, legumes, nuts) per day. Also limit your intake of starches (potatoes and bread) and fats (butter and oils). Doctors recommend that we eat six small meals a day. This ignites the metabolism, provides brain food, and promotes a steady emotional state.

Another key is to balance your activities between work and play. Work may be essential for a living but don't make it your life. Take up a hobby. Walk outdoors; breathe deeply. Even developing a sense of humor adds play into the day. Nurture your rest and sleep habits. Relaxation techniques, meditation, and good, sound sleep are building blocks that add to the foundation of health.

Finally, never forget that you choose your attitude. A positive attitude rises to the challenge

>> **adding quality** to your life

- **Be proactive** in balancing healthy nutrition, activity, and rest.

- **Select fresh seasonal foods**. Divide your plate in two. Fill one half of it with fruits or vegetables. Then split the other half between a protein and a serving of starch.

- **Balance work with play**. Find a hobby and your funny bone. Cherish family and friends. Get outdoors. Take time to rest and recharge.

- **Protect and nurture** a positive outlook. See how it helps you deal with life's challenges and "failed experiments."

of discouragement and changing circumstances, Aggressively preserve your positive outlook; seek out positive people. And acknowledge the big picture of life, with its cycle of peaks and valleys.

The perfect hobby presents a challenge and gives an opportunity for mastery outside your regular routine. Taking your stretching to another level, perhaps by joining a yoga class, will challenge you to go farther and find your inner grace and balance. You might be surprised by what you achieve when you "go for it."

useful resources

Taking a proactive stance toward your health care will pay off royally. A comprehensive program of health care entails first getting your own team of health-care practitioners together, as well as organizing your own health-care strategy for healthy living.

Stretching comes under several categories and can be integrated into other programs such as fitness, Pilates, physiotherapy, yoga, and dance. Here are some resources to get you started.

Fitness

American Council on Exercise
AceFitness.org
The American Council on Exercise® is a nonprofit organization committed to enriching quality of life through safe and effective exercise and physical activity. As America's Authority on Fitness, ACE protects the public by setting certification and continuing education standards for fitness professionals.

American College of Sports Medicine
acsm.org
ACSM is devoted to public awareness and education about the benefits of physical activity for people of all ages, from all occupations.

Pilates

Pilates Method Alliance
pilatesmethodalliance.org
The Pilates Method Alliance (PMA) is the international not-for-profit professional association for the Pilates method. The PMA's mission is to protect the public by establishing certification and continuing education standards for Pilates professionals.

Yoga

Iyengar Yoga Association
iyengar-yoga.com
The Iyengar method of yoga is initially learned through the in-depth study of asanas (posture) and pranayama (breath control). Mr. Iyengar has systematized over 200 classical yoga asanas and 14 different types of pranayamas. These have been structured and categorized so as to allow a beginner to progress surely and safely from basic postures to the most advanced as they gain flexibility, strength, and sensitivity in mind, body, and spirit.

Ashtanga Yoga Institute
kpjayi.org
Ashtanga Yoga is an ancient system of yoga that was taught by Vamana Rishi in the *Yoga Korunta*. This text was imparted to Sri T. Krishnamacharya in the early 1900s by his guru Rama Mohan Brahmachari, and was later passed down to Pattabhi Jois.

Anusara Yoga
anusara.com.
Anusara (a-nu-sar-a), means "flowing with grace," "going with the flow," "following your heart." Founded by John Friend in 1997, Anusara Yoga is a powerful hath yoga system that unifies a Tantric philosophy of Intrinsic Goodness with Universal Principles of Alignment™.

Physical therapy

apta.org
The American Physical Therapy Association (APTA) is a national professional organization representing more than 72,000 members. Its goal is to foster

dvancements in physical
therapy practice, research, and
education. Look for its "Find a
PT" section to help you find a PT
in your area.

Nutrition

nutridiary.com
This free online food and exercise
diary will help you analyze and
chart your diet and activity level
so that you can attain your diet
goals. Whether you want to
maintain, lose, or gain weight,
having a goal and keeping track
is a great motivator to stick
with a healthy eating and
exercise program.

drclydewilson.com
Dr. Clyde Wilson is a former
Stanford University instructor and
runs the Sports Medicine
Institute in Palo Alto, California.
He is an expert in human
performance, and his website
offers free downloads on optimal
nutrition for general health as well
as athletic nutrition.

Exercise for postural problems

The following useful DVDs are
published by Suzanne Martin's
company Pilates Therapeutics
LLC (pilatestherapeutics.com).

*Pilates Therapeutics® The Upper
Core: Exercises for a Pain-Free
Life* (2002)
This DVD was developed to
respond to the prevalence of
repetitive stress injuries of the
shoulders, arms, and hands that
have accompanied our increased
use of computers.

*Pilates Therapeutics® The Pelvic
Core: More Exercise for a Pain-
Free Life* (2002)
This DVD focuses on 24
balancing exercises to help low
back and pelvic pain, knee
problems, and post-pregnancy
restoration.

Pilates Therapeutics® The Scoliosis Management Series

*Scoliosis Series Part 1:
Management & Improvement
featuring Wall Springs* (2006)
Part 1 is designed to help
persons who have scoliosis, or
abnormal curvature of the spine.

*Scoliosis Series Part 2:
Breathing Exercises as Part of
Scoliosis Management* (2007)
Part 2 continues the concepts for
managing scoliosis from Part 1,
but focuses on breathing for
long-term management.

Other DVDs by Suzanne Martin

*Pilates Therapeutics® A Step-
Wise Approach to Post-Natal
Restoration* (2007)
This DVD is designed to be of
use to any woman who has given
birth in the last 18 months or will
give birth.

*Pilates Therapeutics® Breast
Cancer Survivor's Guide to
Physical Restoration* (2007)
This DVD is for women who have
had or will have surgeries related
to breast cancer treatment.

Other publications by Suzanne Martin

Stretching
(Dorling Kindersley 2005)
A best-seller, *Stretching* is a
comprehensive guidebook.
Starting with a full-body catalog
of stretches, *Stretching* helps
beginners as well as advanced
stretchers to find the appropriate
routine for individual needs.
Sections include a 3-week
postural program, how to begin
stretching, stretches for everyday
activities and sports, as well as
therapeutic stretches for arms,
and the low back.

Don't miss out on the award-
winning *Stretching Card Deck*
created from the original 2005
edition.

15 Minute Better Back Workout
(Dorling Kindersley 2008)
Better Back has four 15-minute
workouts based on the Pilates
Method. Each section has 12
exercises that are explained in
detail with photography and text
as well as demonstrated on an
included DVD. Each section
consists of a warm-up, and
specific abdominal and back
exercises.

To contact Suzanne Martin
totalbodydevelopment.com

>> **15** minute

PILATES

WORKOUT

>> **author** foreword

This collection of four Pilates programs is meant as a tool, to teach, guide, and inform and, hopefully, to inspire. The programs will excite your body and mind into action and launch you into a lifetime of wellness and health.

Pilates is not "just another workout." Pilates goes where you do. It's a mindset, a perspective, and a lifestyle. Approached in that way, Pilates guarantees results.

When I first signed on to this project, I was overwhelmed by the possibilities. Where to begin, I thought? Oddly, it was my practice of Pilates that gave me the wherewithal to accomplish the job. Pilates exercises are finite—or so I had been taught—in the same way as there has to be a finite number of words and images in this book. But the beauty of Pilates is that the more intimately you know the system, the more complex and fascinating it becomes. If you truly understand the method, you will always have the perfect exercise at your fingertips without having to beg, borrow, or steal from any other method or technique. Everything you need is right there. By drawing on what I have learned over the 25 years I have been a student of Pilates, I have composed a novel approach to a brilliant and timeless method of exercise.

This project reignited my passion for Pilates in a whole new way. The constraints imposed upon me became utterly liberating. What a luxury once again to reinvent the familiar. This book takes a new approach—one intended to drive home the mission of Pilates. That is, to get you living a better life—off the floor and out the door.

Here you have four distinct programs that are derivative in nature. By and large, the choreography is pure Pilates. The order of exercises is my own and I believe the sequences to be effective and efficient, which is the hallmark of true Pilates work. Sadly, for the Pilates purist, there is no atlas to serve as a reliable resource for a concrete list of exercises. At best, we are piecing together memories that are subjective and interpretive. I so wish that Joe and Clara Pilates were here to share their gifts with us. I believe they would have been proud to see their work preserved yet progressing after all these years.

>> **how to** use this book

The four 15-minute Pilates programs in this book are the closest you can get to having a personal trainer right by your side. They offer you the flexibility and ease of use that our busy lifestyles demand. These workouts will help you to accomplish your everyday goals for your everyday life!

I am a huge fan of clichés. One that comes to mind when considering how best to approach these programs is, "Be prepared, or be prepared to fail." The biggest mistake you can make is to dive into the material without reading through this book and watching the DVD. Pilates can be tricky. Exercises may appear to focus on one area but actually are intended to accomplish something different.

There are several tools to help you understand the details. The DVD is designed to be used with the book to reinforce the exercises shown there. As you watch the DVD, page references to the book flash up on the screen. Refer to these pages for more detailed instruction.

On each page, the photographs capture the essence of the exercises in simple step-by-step images. Some exercises require two or three images, while others only require one. Certain exercises contain smaller inset photos that depict the first step. You will also find targeted "feel-it-here" graphics on specific exercises. These are intended to emphasize the fact that there is always a different area of the body to focus on.

The gatefolds

If I had a nickel for every time a client asked me if we had a chart of the Pilates exercises; well, you can figure out the rest! Lucky for you, at the end of each program, a gatefold chart of the exercises follows. These are meant to provide at-a-glance reminders. You won't be able to learn how to do the exercises from the gatefolds since we have

pared down the images there, providing only one or two per exercise as your reminder. But once you have watched the DVD, read through the book, and practiced each move thoroughly, these gatefolds will become invaluable. For tips on how often to perform the programs and how to combine them for longer workouts, see pp. 240–241.

The gatefolds At-a-glance charts will help further your practice once you no longer need the step-by-step images. Review the full program before beginning.

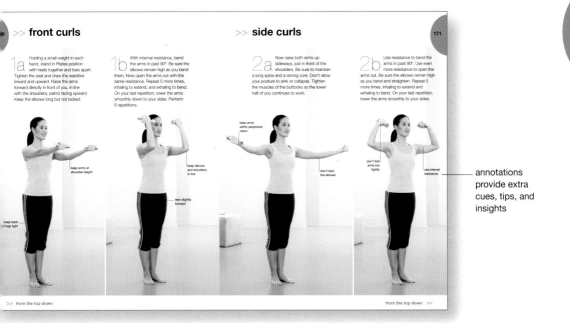

1a Holding a small weight in each hand, stand in Pilates position with heels together and toes apart. Tighten the seat and draw the waistline inward and upward. Raise the arms forward directly in front of you, in line with the shoulders, palms facing upward. Keep the elbows long but not locked.

1b With internal resistance, bend the arms in past 90°. Be sure the elbows remain high as you bend them. Now open the arms out with the same resistance. Repeat 5 more times, inhaling to extend, and exhaling to bend. On your last repetition, lower the arms smoothly down to your sides. Perform 6 repetitions.

2a Now raise both arms up sideways, just in front of the shoulders. Be sure to maintain a long spine and a strong core. Don't allow your posture to sink or collapse. Tighten the muscles of the buttocks so the lower half of you continues to work.

2b Use resistance to bend the arms in past 90°. Use even more resistance to open the arms out. Be sure the elbows remain high as you bend and straighten. Repeat 5 more times, inhaling to extend and exhaling to bend. On your last repetition, lower the arms smoothly to your sides.

keep arms at shoulder-height

keep elbows and shoulders in line

lean slightly forward

keep back of legs tight

keep arms within peripheral vision

don't lock the elbows

don't fold arms too tightly

use internal resistance

annotations provide extra cues, tips, and insights

>> from the top down

from the top down >>

the step-by-steps Work from left to right as you follow the step-by-step exercises. Be certain you understand the beginning and end position before progressing.

the gatefold shows all the main steps of the program

5a ▲ Rowing 2 page 221

5b ▲ Rowing 2 page 221

6a ▲ Spine Twist page 222

6b ▲ Spine Twist page 222

7a ▲ The Saw page 223

7b ▲ The Saw page 223

...ge 220

10b ▲ Thigh Stretch page 226

11 ▲ Footwork 1 page 227

12 ▲ Footwork 2 page 227

13 ▲ Footwork 3 page 228

14 ▲ Tendon Stretch page 228

15 ▲ Front Splits page 229

16 ▲ Side Splits page 229

>> **what you need** to start

People spend so much time getting ready to exercise that many never actually do it. I have a button that reads, "I'm in no shape to exercise." This is an unfortunate and all-too common sentiment. Contrary to popular belief it is unnecessary to prepare for exercise. You simply must decide to begin.

You will need nothing more than some 2-pound (1 kg) hand weights and a well padded mat. Since some rolling exercises can cause bruising on an unpadded surface, many yoga mats may be unsuitable. Instead, choose a mat specifically for Pilates. Finally, keep a towel handy as well as some water, and you'll be ready to go.

Clothing is next. I once had a client with knock knees who happened to be wearing pants with a seam down the front of the legs. Without thinking, I asked her to position her legs so that the seam was perfectly straight. Voilà! Her legs were better aligned and most importantly, she could see it herself. Whenever possible, select clothing with stripes or visible seams. You'll immediately notice asymmetries and will naturally correct them.

Pilates is normally performed barefoot. However, studios and health clubs often institute a footwear requirement. Bare feet are fine for the home, but fo other settings, look for socks with grips to reduce slippage and protect your feet. There are even socks with compartments for each toe. Whatever you select, be sure to avoid slippery socks or cumbersome shoes that might reduce foot mobilit

Where to work out

The single largest impediment to any exercise program is inconvenience, so find yourself an area

A proper Pilates mat, a hand towel, and some small han weights (2 lb/1 kg) are all you need to begin these Pilates programs. Be sure you have a clear space to work out in.

...hat is easy to get to and a time that is convenient ...or your schedule. Pilates can be done anywhere ...ou have enough room to stretch out on a mat. ...ou can practice at a gym or at home. You can ...ven practice on a lawn or beach, as long as you ...ave an appropriate mat.

...he safety instinct

...ave you ever heard a little voice inside your head ...autioning you to stop what you were doing? Did ...ou listen? If you did, you are probably naturally ...ntuitive about safety. For the rest of us, developing ...hat intuition will be largely trial and error. To keep ...ou working out safely, here are some guidelines:

- Begin with just one program.
- Remember to hydrate. By the time you feel ...hirsty, you are already dehydrated.
- Learn to distinguish between effort and pain. ...ffort is OK, pain is a signal to stop.
- If something doesn't "feel" right, stop.

Clothing can be a visual aid as you work out. Selecting attire with stripes can help you establish good alignment and make improvements to your form.

>> **tips for** getting started

- **Don't waste time** getting ready to exercise. You are ready. Just begin.

- **If a mat is not readily available** use some folded blankets or large towels instead. Plush carpeting can also be a suitable workout surface.

- **Find a time of day** when your energy is at its lowest. Just lying down for one exercise will get your blood flowing and will give you an energy burst.

>> **pilates** from the inside out

Therapists train their patients to become self-aware. This is a significant step toward mental and emotional well-being. Similarly, exercise instructors teach you to become physically self-aware. By recognizing your habits and body mechanics, you can embark upon a path of physical health and well-being.

Your body is amazing. The coordination of events required for simple actions such as bending your knee or opening your hand is astonishing, yet they happen without us noticing a thing.

By contrast, Pilates teaches your mind to train your body very consciously. During the programs you will continually be required to recognize your positions, make adjustments and note your physical sensations. In addition, you must also be focused on the order of exercises, so that you can anticipate and prepare for the next move.

This "mind–body" connection often suggests a workout that is neither physical nor rigorous, but Pilates is both. Just because we think our way through Pilates does not make it less taxing on the muscles. In fact, just the opposite is true. In the words of the late Frederick Schiller, "It is the mind itself that builds the body." Joseph Pilates was quite fond of this saying.

Learning new patterns

Our brains are built to learn new patterns. As we learn new skills, connections between previously unconnected brain cells are formed. Repetition is key. Each time you do a correct abdominal curl you are building a connection that makes it easier to do correctly the next time. In sum, "cells that fire together, wire together."

Pilates trains this mind-to-body dialog. You will learn to direct your actions on a gross motor scale as well as a fine motor scale so your results will be amplified and expedited.

>> **just make it** happen

- **Pay attention to your body** throughout your day. Self-awareness is key to good health. If you watch how you move, your exercise routine will improve.

- **Exercise is an activity.** It is not something that happens to you—you make it happen.

- **It requires more energy to avoid** something than simply to do it. Don't waste any time making excuses. Just hit the mat and get started!

Your Pilates body

As you read this book and progress through the workouts, you will find instructions for and mentions of specific parts of your body. The chart opposite is a handy reference guide to them. For ease of use, we have chosen layperson terms rather than anatomical ones. Names and labels allow your mind to grasp more effectively what is required of you, so become familiar with them and use them as you move through your workout. Think of the chart as a map for your mind.

Remember these simple names for your body parts. Learning about your anatomy will help you identify trouble spots as well as areas of strength in your body.

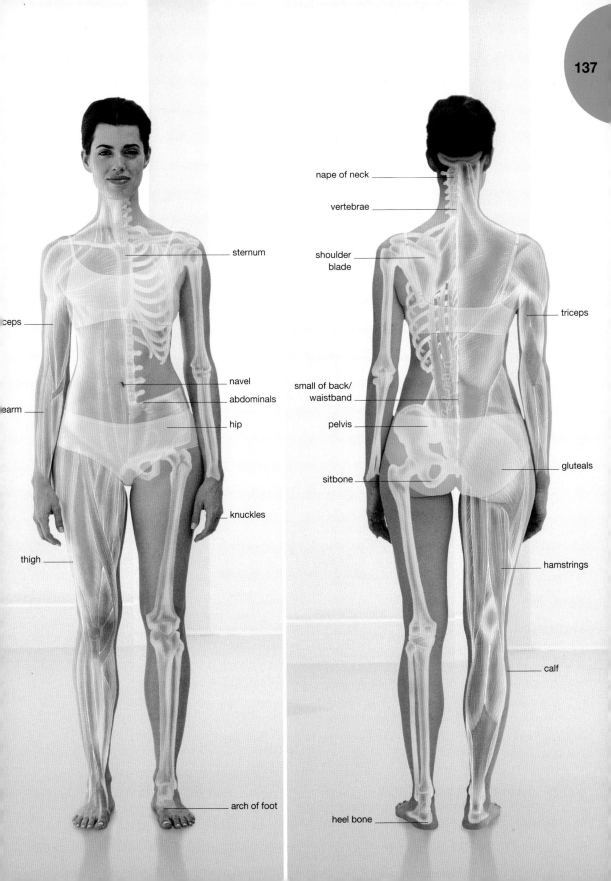

sternum

nape of neck

vertebrae

shoulder
blade

ceps

triceps

navel

abdominals

small of back/
waistband

earm

hip

pelvis

gluteals

sitbone

knuckles

thigh

hamstrings

calf

arch of foot

heel bone

>> **pilates** concepts

Your Pilates technique and form can constantly be improved upon. Just as musicians must rehearse tirelessly, Pilates will only get better as you train. Think of it as a language. First you learn the words, then some phrases, and finally you work on your accent. Let's begin here with your first Pilates words.

Before you can start on the mechanics of Pilates, there are six fundamental principles that you should become familiar with. These principles give substance and purpose to the workouts and help you learn to integrate your workout into your life so you begin to feel healthy and strong. Remember, the benefits of Pilates are meant to extend well beyond the actual workout.

Control

This is the primary principle of the system. In his time, Mr. Pilates called his method "Contrology." His focus on controlled movement was a result of his years of blending Eastern and Western disciplines. As you work out, control your muscles, your positions, and your tempos. Your body is your tool and by exerting control over it, it will produce better and better results.

Centering

This is a somewhat vague principle to many people. The idea is that all movement begins from your center. I'm of the mind that Pilates was really drawing on the principle that you must "stabilize before you mobilize." In Pilates we brace or stabilize the core and then mobilize the limbs. Beyond that, there is an energetic component in working from your center. It's as though you were able to harness and then project out through the limbs all of the energy and activity going on in your internal organs. Centering is akin to saying you should work from the inside out.

>> **tips for** surefire success

- **Don't over-analyze the work.** Pilates is complicated but it's meant to be a moving system. Keep moving at all costs.

- **Working out is an extension of your life.** Put the same effort into it that you would into anything else.

- **Don't work out—work in!** Inner work shapes the outer body.

- **Never say die.** If an exercise is easy, you're not working hard enough.

- **Don't ask what** an exercise is good for. Mr. Pilates said, "It's good for the body."

Concentration

Concentration is key to Pilates. Without focused concentration, any exercise can only be moderately beneficial. Concentration elevates your intensity and so takes your results up to a far higher level.

Precision

This is the fourth principle and just as many of the other principles apply globally, so "precision" serves as an umbrella for this whole list. Attention to the smallest detail is what makes Pilates so effective.

Breath
Breathing is a focus of the Pilates work. Many people come to Pilates because they have heard that it is a breathing technique. You will learn step-by-step breathing in these programs but it is not their focus. As a general rule, inhale to prepare for a movement and exhale as you execute it.

Flow of movement
This is an element that comes later in the practice but can be incorporated early on. As you learn each exercise, be sure to perform it in a seamless, flowing manner. Eventually you'll work on creating one long routine.

Minimum of movement
Other ideas and concepts, such as symmetry, balance, and integration arise as instructors make their own contributions to Pilates. All of these are applicable but Mr. Pilates clearly intended his work to be succinct, so when establishing its main tenets, he chose only the key moves and critical concepts. This working list of six incorporates all the dozens of ideas and concepts at play in Pilates.

Off the floor and out the door
Now that you've learned the six principles, think about how they apply to real life. Concepts such as control, precision, or breath can be applied to your life anywhere and anytime. Your workout should be a microcosm of how you live. If you never did any of these programs, you could still embark upon a brand-new lifestyle simply by incorporating these key principles.

Working out on your own should be just as focused as working with a trainer. Learn to be your own teacher by cueing and correcting yourself constantly.

>> **pilates** top to tail

Now that we've covered the ideology of Pilates and the approach you will need to be successful, let's review the physical principles that are present throughout the programs in this series. Certain elements of positioning are specific to Pilates. Let's start at the top of the body and work our way down.

To keep your neck well aligned during abdominal work, imagine resting your head on a raised support. The curve should be long and natural both front and back. Avoid any crunching or tightening around the throat.

Your breathing in Pilates needs to be specific. The abdominals must work in a contracted fashion at all times so your breathing must be redirected both upward and outward. Be aware that your lungs actually extend all the way above your collarbones. Practice breathing laterally, expanding the rib cage sideways as you inhale, and then contracting it inward as you exhale.

Below the waist

Pilates teachers have several labels for the abdominals, including the core, the center, and frequently, the powerhouse. No matter the tag,

Practice breathing laterally with the hands on either side of the rib cage. On an inhale, the hands should pull apart.

Exhale and feel the ribs narrowing. The hands draw together. Keep the abdominals tight.

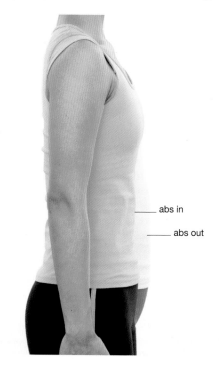

abs in

abs out

The Pilates Scoop activates the abdominal wall. Keep your waist lifted and narrowed. Never allow it to collapse.

our strength and control always spring from the center of your torso. Your powerhouse specifically incorporates your abs, hips, and buttocks as well.

The Pilates Scoop is the signature of the method. Even if you have difficulty pulling the abdominals inward, you must never allow them to push outward.

Optimal spinal alignment means positioning your spine to preserve its natural curves. To do this, when you are lying flat for abdominal exercises, keep from tucking or curling the lower back. Instead, try to lengthen the spine. The end result should be strong, supportive abdominal muscles.

Additionally, when you are working your seat muscles or gluteals, think of "wrapping" the muscles of the buttocks and thighs around toward the back. This will create a tightening and lifting of those muscles and will help to support your spine.

Pilates position or Pilates stance doesn't happen in the feet, although it looks that way. Working from your hips down, the gluteal muscles in your rear-end and in the backs of your thighs work together to rotate and wrap around. This causes a slight opening of the toes.

Perfect the details

As you work out, focus on your symmetry. Imagine your torso in a box from shoulders to hips. If your box is square, you are likely well aligned. You also need to work within your "frame," which means keeping your limbs within your peripheral vision and never going beyond a comfortable joint range.

Never forget that Pilates is strength training. To maximize its benefits you must always work with resistance. Some resistance is provided by gravity and your positions. More important is the internal resistance you create. Your entire Pilates routine should incorporate this internal resistance.

Opposition is a final but vital ingredient of your Pilates practice. For every action there is an equal and opposite reaction. Pilates is the same. As one side reaches, another side contracts. If you lift up, you also anchor down. By using direct opposition you will find the stability and strength in your core to build a better body.

In abdominal work keep your neck lengthened and aligned. Don't force the chin down or tense the throat. Lifting the head comes from your abdominal strength.

Performing exercises on your back can be tricky for your spine. When working your abdominals, keep your spine lengthened rather than curling it up underneath you.

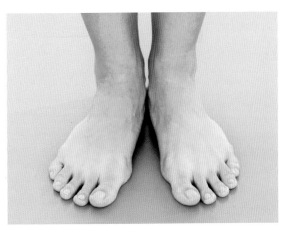

In Pilates stance the heels connect as the toes open. This is achieved by activating and rotating the buttocks muscles and the muscles in the backs of the thighs.

15 minute

Focus on control
Activate your powerhouse
Learn the classic routine

day by **day** >>

>> **day** by **day**

This program is designed to be the first routine you learn. Perform it every day if possible. If you can only commit to one program, this is your best choice. This classical sequence of movements contains all the benefits of the Pilates method and serves as a primer for all of your other programs.

Your goal here is to learn how to move according to the six principles and the physical guidelines of Pilates. We begin the program with some specific abdominal recruitment exercises to get you breathing correctly and also to teach you to use your abdominals effectively. The remainder of the routine is as Mr. Pilates developed it. We end with a rolling exercise which may be challenging at first but will, with practice, be possible.

Starting and finishing
Practice the initiation of each move in several ways. First, scan your body parts for their positions and for any necessary adjustments. Second, before moving anything, take a breath. Finally, brace or activate your center to stabilize your core and free your limbs to do their work.

To end an exercise, linger at the final moment as though you were posing for a photograph, but rather than freezing your body in space, try to exaggerate the important points. Go for a deeper stretch, a longer leg, a more scooped-out midsection. Then you can rest.

Transitions
Weaving your way from one exercise to another with elegance and precision is the goal. The image to the right illustrate proper transitioning through movements. Transition from sitting to lying through a curling-down movement, and from lying to sitting through a curling-up movement. If this is too difficult, simply roll onto your side to get down or up between movements.

To begin with, use this method to transition smoothly. From lying to sitting, roll over onto your side, prop yourself up with your hands, and come up to sitting. From sitting to lying, roll to one side, lower yourself to the mat, and roll onto your back.

If your core is strong enough, transition from sitting up to lying down by curling your tail under you and lowering down to the mat, one vertebra at a time. To rise from a lying exercise to a sitting one, hold behind your knees and curl up without allowing your feet to move.

>> **abs wake-up**

1a Lie flat with your knees bent and your hands across your abdominals. Even lying flat, your posture should be perfect. Keep your neck long, your shoulders down, and your "box" square. Inhale deeply and let your abdominals expand. Your hands will lift as you do this.

press legs together

hands should rise

1b Now exhale completely, emptying the lungs and sinking the abdominals. Don't crunch the midsection or hunch the shoulders. Just pull the belly in deeper, allowing the waist to hollow out. Repeat for 4 repetitions, exhaling longer and contracting deeper with each repetition.

keep ribs in

keep neck long

2a Extend your arms forward so they hover just above the mat. Your feet remain firmly planted on the mat and your legs are pressed together. Your abdominals pull inward and upward. Prepare to curl up by inhaling.

activate abdominals

keep arms above mat

2b Exhale, and without letting your abdominal wall expand, lift your head, neck, and shoulders, curling up off the mat. Reach your arms longer and keep focused on your midsection. Lower down smoothly with an inhale. As you repeat, pull in your abdominals even further. Repeat 3 more times for a total of 4 repetitions.

keep eyes on midsection

sink abs deeper

>> the hundred

3a Begin with both knees drawn into your chest. Curl your upper body up off the mat and reach your arms along your sides just above the mat. Pull in your abdominals.

pull abs in and up

keep hips flat on mat

3b Take both legs up to a 90° angle, with the shins parallel to the floor. Pump the arms up and down vigorously, breathing in for 5 pumps and out for 5 pumps. Continue until you reach 100, resting briefly if needed. Keep the abdominals deep and the torso still and strong.

point knees straight up

keep fingers long

4a Sit upright at the front of your mat, legs apart and feet flat, holding behind your thighs. Inhale and direct he back of your waistband to pull down toward he mat. Your tail will curl underneath and your bdominals will hollow.

draw shoulders down ——

—— lift chest up

4b Keep curling your tail as you aim the small of your back to the floor. Keep your legs still. Pause at your lowest point and take 3 breaths, hollowing your abdominals further. Exhale and fold back up. Roll up to your tallest posture and repeat one more set.

feel it here

fold in the waist

>> single-leg circles

5a Lie flat with both your legs and arms extended. Fold your right leg in and straighten it to the sky. Fix the rest of your body solidly on the mat, stretching both knees and pressing your shoulders back and down. Cross your raised leg up and over your body, aiming for your left shoulder.

lift leg and cross it over

press triceps down

5b Continue making a circle with the raised leg, around and back up to center. Circle 4 more times, then reverse for another 5 repetitions. Bend the knee in, lower it, and repeat to the left side.

keep hip of bottom leg stable

keep bottom leg straight

6a Sit at the front edge of your mat, holding behind your thighs with your legs in the [air]. Keep your shins parallel to the floor. [H]old your chest high and scoop your [a]bdominals. Your elbows are open wide [a]nd your ankles are long.

keep knees and feet in a line

keep abs scooped in

6b Tip your pelvis under you, then use your abs to ease back further. At your limit, [draw] your abs in further and fold your waist [by] rounding forward. Sit tall and repeat 3 [mo]re times. Lower your feet only after the [last] repetition.

curl tail under

hollow out midsection

>> **single-leg stretch**

7a Lie flat with both knees bent into your chest. Before you curl up, be sure your box or frame is square and then activate your powerhouse.

hug knees tightly

keep chest open

7b Curl the upper body off the mat and hold the left leg, reaching the left hand to the ankle and the other to the knee. Extend the right leg 45°. Control the torso as you switch legs, inhaling on one side and exhaling on the other. Continue switching for 8 repetitions. Bend both knees to finish. Rest the head.

watch hand placement

reach leg long

8 Curl the upper body back up and hug the ankles in tightly. Inhale to simultaneously reach the arms and legs forward. Exhale to hug them back in. Keep the upper body lifted off the mat and repeat for 4 more repetitions.

take legs to 45° angle

hold arms at hip height

9 Repeat as before but now add a backward reaching of the arms. Hollow the abs even deeper as you repeat the sequence. The arms and legs now reach to a 45° angle. Repeat 5 times and rest.

take arms to 45° angle

tighten the abs

>> spine stretch forward

10a

Sit tall at the front of your mat with your feet just wider than the mat. Extend both arms in front of you at shoulder height and flex your feet. Tighten your rear-end and inhale so you feel as though you are rising up off the mat.

press shoulders down

point toes u

10b

Exhale slowly and dive over, lowering your head and reaching forward with your arms to stretch your back. As you round, keep pulling back in your waist. Inhale to return to upright. Repeat 3 more times. After the final repetition, exaggerate your height, lengthening even taller.

dive head through arms

pull back in the waist

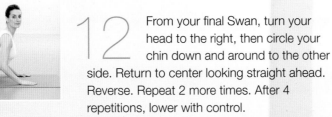

11 Lie face down with legs together and hands under your shoulders. Breathing normally, lengthen your spine forward, pressing your shoulders back away from your ears. Continue lengthening to arc up off the mat. Use your stomach muscles to support you. Lower with control. Repeat 2 more times.

legs may separate

take elbows to 90° angle

12 From your final Swan, turn your head to the right, then circle your chin down and around to the other side. Return to center looking straight ahead. Reverse. Repeat 2 more times. After 4 repetitions, lower with control.

stretch the neck

keep weight centered

>> child's pose/pelvic lift

13 Push back to sit on your heels with your back rounded, hands in front of you. Open your knees slightly to allow your upper body to sink deeper. Keep your abdominals lifted as you take 3 deep breaths. With each inhale, try to stretch and release your lower-back muscles. With each exhale, draw your navel even higher upward. After 3 deep breaths, roll up to a kneeling position.

reach hands forward

knees may open

14 Lie with knees bent and legs hip-width apart. Feel your chest open, shoulders back, and spine long. Inhale and raise your hips without arching your back. Exhale and lower down, one vertebra at a time. Repeat 3 more times, increasing the articulation of your spine each time.

feel it here

reach knees forwa

keep ribs in

>> rolling like a ball

15a

Balance on your sitbones at the front edge of your mat, hugging your ankles into your body and nestling your head between your knees. Without letting your feet touch down, tuck your tail under you and begin to roll back.

hold ankles snugly

keep head tucked in

15b

Keep rolling through your spine back to your shoulder blades, then return to the starting point. Use your abdominals for control, especially on the return. Try not to skip any sections of your spine. Repeat 5 more times, inhaling as you roll and exhaling as you return.

take feet close to buttocks

aim sitbones to the sky

don't rock onto neck

3a

▲ **The Hundred**
page 148

3b

▲ **The Hundred** page 148

page 147

page 2 page 153

10a

▲ **Spine
Stretch
Forward**
page 154

10b

Spine Stretch Forward page 154

ummary day by day

▲ **Abs Wake-up** page 146

▲ **Abdominal Curls** page 147

▲ **Abdominal Curls**

▲ **Single-leg Stretch** page 152

▲ **Double-leg Stretch 1** page 153

▲ **Double-leg Stretc**

day by day program >>

5 minute **summary**

page 150

▲ **Rolling
Preparation**
page 151

▲ **Rolling Preparation** page 151

▲ **Rolling like a
Ball** page 157

▲ **Rolling like a Ball** page 157

5a

▲ **Single-leg
Circles**
page 150

▲ **The Roll-down** page 149

Roll-
n
149

▲ **Single-leg Circles**

13

▲ **Child's Pose**
page 156

Swan
155

▲ **Neck Roll** page 155

▲ **Pelvic Lift** page 1

>> **day by day** extras

The most important thing about this program is making sure you do it. Once you have the routine memorized, it will take less time and effort to perform. To help you commit the order to memory, try writing the names of the exercises down or singing them along to a familiar tune.

>> **Checklist**

Be sure to scan your moves for evidence of the six principles at work. The choreography of each move is less important than the quality of those movements.

• Did you transition smoothly between exercises using minimal movement while you were performing this program?

• Have you accomplished the "scoop" of the abdominals to draw the muscles inward instead of distending them?

• When curling up, were you able to contract the abdominals fully without allowing any pushing outward?

• During the Hundred did you manage to keep your upper body fixed at one height, resisting any shaking in the body?

• For the Single-Leg Circles, the hips must remain stable. Were you able to accomplish this?

• Were you able to isolate the pelvis in the Rolling Preparation so that no other body parts were moving?

• The Spine Stretch Forward should be performed as though your body were fixed against a wall and the upper back were peeling away from it. Did you feel that?

• The Pelvic Lift is a variation of a Pilates equipment exercise known as the Breathing. Were you able to articulate your spine fully as you lowered your hips back to the mat?

• Rolling like a Ball is an exercise in control. Are you able to sustain your balance momentarily between each repetition?

Modify/Adjust

It will benefit you more to perfect your form in a less advanced move than to force your body past its comfort zone. Modify as necessary.

• Change the bottom leg to a bent-knee position during the Single-Leg Circles.

• Alter your position to separate the legs slightly when lying on your stomach to alleviate lower-back pressure.

• Lower the head to avoid neck strain during exercises where the head is raised.

• Hold behind your knees rather than around the ankles in Rolling like a Ball.

Challenge

As you incorporate challenges, do so incrementally. This workout is meant to stay with you for a lifetime.

• Remember to linger at the end of each exercise to perfect your position even more for optimal results.

• Try to increase the resistance by creating internal pressure in your muscles as they push and pull against gravity.

• Vary the tempo to go slower during the hardest parts of each exercise—don't throw it away.

• Work to extend the legs a bit lower yet still remain scooped during the Single- and Double-Leg Stretch.

• Use the curling-up transition rather than rolling through one side.

Trainer tips

The goal of this program is to get you acquainted with your body. Focus your attention to problem areas within exercises.

• Connectivity is key. Stop moving between exercises and your body forgets that it is working out. No matter what—keep moving.

• Every movement has a countermovement, so if you twist your torso you'll find one side is pulling backward while the other pulls forward. Pay attention to these naturally opposing moments in each exercise.

• When curling up, imagine four points at your ribs and hips and draw them together, sinking your abdominals.

15 minute

from the
top down >>

Focus on centering
Activate your Pilates box
Learn Pilates with weights

>> **from the** top down

This program is comprised of standing exercises and is performed almost entirely with hand weights. I've structured the routine to show that Pilates is not confined to the mat. The program you are about to do not only gets you upright, but also trains you to carry this work with you wherever you go.

We begin by standing for a series of arm and upper-body exercises, performed in Pilates stance. Then you move on to a flat-back series, which challenges your core, coordination, and alignment, before coming upright again. Now the fun begins. The next set of exercises requires you to be utterly stable in movements that are targeted to bend you, shift you, and shake you. You'll close the routine with some modified Pilates Push-ups and a historical breathing exercise—The Windmill.

Starting and finishing

To start off, you will need to establish a solid standing Pilates stance. The hamstrings will wrap tightly around the back and the buttocks will tense. For standing exercises in Pilates, there is a bit of an incline in the body. It's often described as "leaning into the wind." The position requires you to shift your weight slightly forward toward the fronts, or balls, of the feet. You will sustain this position for each upright move in the program.

At the end of this program, we take a breathing reminder from a vintage exercise. Mr. Pilates developed a small handheld device for improving breath control during the exercise. Today, we do it without but must remember to challenge our lungs to empty every drop of air before inhaling again.

Transitions

Linking the hand-weight exercises requires keeping your torso strong and stable and the arms moving fluidly. In the flat-back series, move from your flat

>> **secrets** of success

- **Use the Side Bends exercise** to emphasize opposition. As you reach up and away, anchor the opposite side of the body down into the ground.

- **Push-ups are a great move** for working on spinal alignment. Once in your "plank" position, arrange your spine in one solid line from your hips to the top of your head.

- **Baby Circles** reinforce the idea of stability before mobility. The temptation to waver and vacillate as you circle must be resisted at all costs.

back into a rounded spine as though you were melting over your legs. From your lowest stretch, roll back up through your spine. In this series you will be shifting your body weight from upright, to bent over to rounded over. No matter your body position, keep your weight centered through the middle of your feet. Don't sink back in the heels or rise up on the toes. Like all Pilates movements, these transitions are mindful and precise.

From the Top Down seems to focus on the upper body only. With practice, though, it becomes clear that every Pilates exercise is a full-body experience.

>> **front curls**

1a Holding a small weight in each hand, stand in Pilates position with heels together and toes apart. Tighten the seat and draw the waistline inward and upward. Raise the arms forward directly in front of you, in line with the shoulders, palms facing upward. Keep the elbows long but not locked.

1b With internal resistance, bend the arms in past 90°. Be sure the elbows remain high as you bend them. Now open the arms out with the same resistance. Repeat 5 more times, inhaling to extend, and exhaling to bend. On your last repetition, lower the arms smoothly down to your sides. Perform 6 repetitions.

keep arms at shoulder-height

keep elbo and shou in line

lean slightly forward

keep back of legs tight

2a Now raise both arms up sideways, just in front of the shoulders. Be sure to maintain a long spine and a strong core. Don't allow your posture to sink or collapse. Tighten the muscles of the buttocks so the lower half of you continues to work.

2b Use resistance to bend the arms in past 90°. Use even more resistance to open the arms out. Be sure the elbows remain high as you bend and straighten. Repeat 5 more times, inhaling to extend and exhaling to bend. On your last repetition, lower the arms smoothly to your sides.

keep arms within peripheral vision

don't lock the elbows

don't fold arms too tightly

use internal resistance

>> zip-ups

3a Still holding the small weights, rotate the backs of the hands toward each other so the knuckles face each other. Scoop the abdominals up, tighten the backs of the legs, and shift the weight a tiny bit forward toward the fronts of the feet. Keep the heels flat as you do this. Inhale to prepare.

3b Exhale, open your elbows wide, and pull the weights up under your chin, keeping your neck long and your shoulders relaxed. Lower the weights back down as though you were pushing something heavy away from you. Repeat 5 more times, inhaling to lift and exhaling to lower.

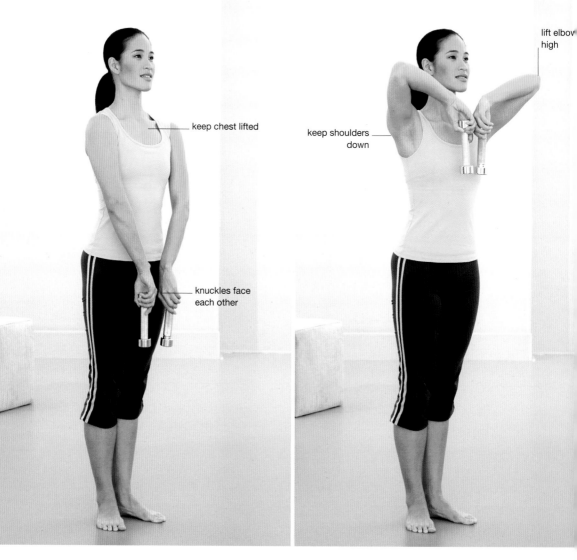

keep chest lifted

knuckles face each other

keep shoulders down

lift elbow high

4a Still holding the weights, place both of them behind your head at the nape of your neck. Tip your chin down slightly and be sure to keep your elbows open wide. Your feet remain in Pilates position with your legs pressed together tightly. Incline your body forward as though you were leaning into the wind."

4b Without locking the elbows, extend the arms overhead. Hold the powerhouse strong and keep the fingers of each hand in contact with each other. Lower with resistance. Repeat 5 more times, exhaling to extend and inhaling to lower.

keep hands close

tip chin down

keep ribs in

don't expand rib cage

>> the boxing

5a Open the feet into parallel, hip-width apart, and stand tall holding the weights. Bend both knees deeply and fold over the legs with a long flat back. Tuck the arms in by your sides, keeping the elbows tight to the body. Lift the abdominals without disrupting your posture. Inhale to prepare.

5b Exhale and simultaneously extend the right arm forward and the left arm back in a boxinglike movement. Inhale to fold the arms back in. Continue, creating resistance and alternating sides for 3 full sets. Complete a total of 6 repetitions. To finish, round over the legs, stretching the back and legs. Slowly roll back up to standing.

angle sitbones back

tuck weights by shoulders

hold abs lifted

don't sit back into heels

6a Start by standing tall, holding the weights, and with legs parallel. Bend your knees and fold over, keeping your spine long and flat. Frame your arms in a circle directly underneath you, bringing your fists toward each other. Lift your powerhouse and inhale to prepare.

6b Exhale and lift both arms to the sides of the room. Don't allow your body position to change as you do this. Inhale and lower your arms as though you were squeezing something together. Perform 2 more repetitions, then reverse your breathing and exhale to prepare for an additional 3 repetitions. Finally, round over your legs to release the spine.

bend knees deeply

make arms frame an oval

keep arms in line with back

feel it here

>> **triceps**

7a Holding the weights, stand tall with your legs parallel. Fold at your waist over your legs and tuck your arms in by your sides. Bring your elbows up a little higher than your back. Activate your abdominals and inhale to begin.

7b Exhale and extend both arms behind you, holding strong in your center. Fold them back in slowly and with control, as though you were pulling something toward you. Repeat 5 more times. Stretch over your legs again before rolling up through your spine, one vertebra at a time.

bring elbows just
above spine

eyes to
the floor

tighten
triceps

keep knees
deeply bent

>> baby circles

8a Standing in Pilates stance, hold your weights just in front of your legs on a slight angle. Shift your weight toward the fronts of your feet, leaning lightly forward and tightening your gluteal muscles. Begin circling the arms 8 times, raising your arms higher with each circle until you are reaching overhead.

8b Reverse your circles, lowering down for 8 circles. Repeat another full set. Try not to shake or bounce your body as you circle your arms. Hold your torso strong and breathe naturally.

arms in an oval

hold weights so they face each other

don't extend arms fully

hold strong in your center

>> lunges

9a Holding the weights, stand with your feet in a "Y," nestling the heel of your left foot into the arch of the right. Angle your body toward your left foot, holding the weights just in front of your thighs. Tighten the backs of your legs and draw your waist in and up. In a fencinglike motion, shoot your left leg out into a deep lunge position as your arms rise quickly up.

9b Shift back onto your straight leg, dragging your left foot back to your right foot as you lower your arms. Repeat 3 more times and switch sides.

palms face forward

feel it here

keep back heel down

keep both legs straight

10a Stand in Pilates stance and extend the right arm up toward the ceiling, hugging the arm against the side of the head. Inhale and lift even higher, arcing up and over to the left.

10b Bend up and away, reaching further over and allowing the bottom arm to hang loosely. Now return to the centerline, resisting on the way up. Lower the arm down by your side and repeat to the left side. Perform 2 more sets for a total of 6 repetitions.

keep shoulder down

arm floats loosely

reach up strongly

feel it here

don't collapse waist

>> push-ups

11a Stand upright in Pilates stance, tightening the backs of your legs. Reach your arms overhead for a breath, then dive over your legs, reaching for the floor and keeping your abdominals lifting. Walk your hands out until you are in a plank position and bend your knees up.

keep hips down

keep hands under shoulders

11b Open your elbows and lower your upper body up and down for 3 push-ups. Straighten your legs behind you, tuck your toes under, and lift your hips, pressing back into your heels for a stretch. Carefully walk your hands back to your legs, stretch a moment, and roll back up to standing. Repeat 1 more set for a total of 6 push-ups.

tighten buttocks muscles

keep neck and head aligned

>> **windmill**

2a Stand tall and envision your spine as a wheel as you inhale. Exhale, tucking your head down and folding over your legs. Try to keep your weight shifted slightly forward. Continue exhaling and rounding your spine down in a curling motion.

12b When you are folded over and have no air left, slowly inhale and uncurl the spine, rolling back up to standing. Repeat 2 more times, exhaling progressively longer each time. Finally, roll the shoulders back, lengthen the neck, and stand tall.

let head hang heavy

keep your hips forward

lift your abs

keep weight on your toes

▲ **Side Curls** page 171　　　　▲ **Zip-ups** page 172　　　　▲ **Zip-ups** page 172

▲ **Baby Circles** page 177　　　　▲ **Lunges** page 178　　　　▲ **Lunges** page 178

summary from the top down

1a	**1b**	**2a**
▲ **nt Curls** page 170	▲ **Front Curls** page 170	▲ **Side Curls** page 171

7a	**7b**	**8a**
▲ **eps** page 176	▲ **Triceps** page 176	▲ **Baby Circles** page 177

from the top down >>

5 minute **summary**

▲ **The Boxing** page 174

▲ **The bug** page 175

▲ **The Bug** page 175

▲ **Windmill** page 181

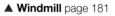
▲ **Windmill** page 181

▲ **Salutes** page 173   ▲ **Salutes** page 173   ▲ **The Boxing** page 174

▲ **Push-ups** page 180

▲ **Side Bend** page 179   ▲ **Side Bend** page 179   ▲ **Push-ups** page 18

>> **from the top down** extras

It's easy to feel the pull of resistance when you do this routine, which involves working with weights. As an experiment, once you've performed this program, do a run-through without any weights but force your muscles to behave as though you were still holding them. This is the essence of internal resistance.

>> Checklist

Remember to move from your center. Although these exercises appear to be for the limbs, they are just as much for your core.

• Did you work within your "frame"—keeping your arms within your peripheral vision?

• Have you worked with internal resistance throughout each movement of the program?

• Can you feel how the lower body must stabilize in order to mobilize the upper body?

• During the Front Curls, as in all Pilates standing positions, were you positioned very slightly forward on your feet as though you were "leaning into the wind?"

• For the Side Curls, were you able to keep pressing the shoulders down using the muscles of your back?

• Are you able to maintain your vertical alignment during the Zip-ups and Salutes so that your spine does not waver?

• Some of the hand-weight exercises are done in parallel. Can you keep your legs aligned so that your feet, knees, and hips are all pointing straight forward?

• Did you remember to keep some weight on the outside foot while side-bending away from that leg?

• The Lunges can be tricky with respect to timing. Did you coordinate the return of the leg and the lowering of the arms so that they end simultaneously?

>> ## Modify/Adjust

Hand weights add another element to your workout. Be sure to work deliberately and carefully through each section.

• Change the angle of the limbs to reduce your range of motion for the arm-weight exercises to make them slightly easier.

• Alter your position if you must, bending the knees less deeply during the flat-back exercises to reduce the intensity.

• Remember to decrease your weights or eliminate them as necessary if undue strain occurs.

>> ## Challenge

You can make an exercise harder by increasing your repetitions or slowing down your tempo. You can also focus on the exacting detail of each move for a real challenge.

• Learn to hold your body still regardless of the movement of the circling arms while you perform the Baby Circles.

• Practice the Lunges focusing on the drag-in to work on activating that hard-to-reach area, the inner thighs.

• Try to increase the weights by a pound or two (0.5 to 1 kg) as you improve. Don't go above 4 to 5 pounds (1.8 to 2.25 kg) total.

>> ## Trainer tips

Work the transitions. Make your connecting movements every bit as important as the main exercises.

• Be sure your breathing is focused and targeted. Always inhale to prepare and exhale as you execute a movement.

• Work with the joint. Be careful not to lock or jam your elbows or knees as you move through the series. Remember that your muscles move your bones, not the other way around.

• As you perform your hand-weight series, aim to keep your wrists in an elongated hold. Extending the wrists long provides increased stability to your forearms as opposed to bending or cocking the wrists and weakening your grip on the weights.

15 minute

Focus on precision
Activate your Pilates stance
Learn the Side Kicks series

from the
bottom up >>

>> **from the** bottom up

This program begins with some preparatory moves and concludes, as does the last program, with an upright exercise. It will build stamina and emphasize centering. By now you should begin to feel comfortable executing the exercises without sacrificing either your form or the key concepts.

We begin with two exercises of my own design that use the Pilates stance with the legs extended in a non-weight-bearing position. We then move into a side-lying position for the classic Pilates Side-Kicks series. Transferring to a seated position, we'll perform a modified Teaser—the "poster pose" for Pilates exercises. This version is meant to work your abdominals and challenge your control as you descend from the pose. The routine rounds out with some moves taken from the Pilates equipment, namely the Hug and the Standing Arm Circles. In between, you'll find the Mermaid, an exercise which embodies the grace and fluidity of the Pilates system.

Starting and finishing

As you sit on the mat at the start with your legs outstretched, forget about the muscles you are planning to work. Begin by activating all the other muscle groups. Sit with tall posture, a lifted waist, and a long neck. As you adjust your body to get ready for Pilates stance, take note of how much should be done in preparation for each exercise.

The final exercise, Arm Circles, is done standing in this program. Although Arm Circles are traditionally performed on Pilates equipment, this variation gets you off the floor and ready for real life.

Transitions

Here, the links between exercises are more complex than before. Approach the Side Kicks Preparation as a position of stability. If you are

> >> **secrets of** success
>
> - **Pilates stance** is initiated from the buttocks. To do this correctly when sitting, draw the buttocks muscles together. You should then rise slightly off your mat.
>
> - **During the up/down** in the Side Kicks, pay special attention to the tempo changes. The leg travels up loosely but lowers down with increasing resistance.
>
> - **The Mermaid** is a lengthening exercise, not a bending one. Be sure not to collapse into your waist. Instead pull up out of your bottom half as though you were being lifted up by your upper arm.

properly positioned you should require very little adjusting. As you progress, resist relaxing your leg in between moves, but stay controlled, using the end of one exercise as the start of the next. When you transfer onto the stomach for the Beats, use minimal movement. Although the Teaser's focus is in its second half, don't ignore your form in the first. This program synthesizes all you have learned.

The Mermaid is a classic Pilates exercise. By anchoring the lower half of the body, the upper half is free to lengthen and stretch.

>> **pilates stance 1 & 2**

1 Sit tall with your legs in front of you, pressing your inner thighs together and keeping your feet long. Place your hands on the outside of your thighs and squeeze your bottom, rotating your legs and feet so they are slightly open. Continue to tighten your buttocks muscles, returning your legs and feet to parallel. Perform a total of 5 repetitions.

keep shoulders back

feel the move with your hands

2 Lie on your back, legs upward, heels together, and toes apart. Tighten your buttocks and rotate your legs slightly out. Use your hands to cue your muscles to work from your hips. Rotate your legs back to parallel. Repeat 4 more times.

keep legs together

lift the chest

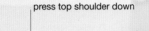

3a Lie on your right side at the back edge of your mat. Prop your head up with your hand, resting on your elbow, and place your left hand in front of your powerhouse. Keeping your chest lifted, pull your abdominals in firmly and lift both legs up in the air, squeezing them tightly.

press top shoulder down

squeeze the backs of the legs

3b Without disrupting your posture, carry your legs forward to the front edge of the mat and lower them with control. You should be at a 45° angle on the mat, with your hips and shoulders stacked one on top of the other.

legs at 45° angle

ke elbow to edge of mat

>> side kicks front

4a Lying on your side at a 45° angle on the mat, elevate your left leg and slightly rotate it up to the ceiling. Your right foot remains solidly on the mat, slightly flexed and pressing down into the floor. Carry your leg forward in a kicking motion, pulsing twice at the height of your kick.

pull the top hip back

don't rotate the bottom leg

4b Sweep the leg down and back behind the body, tightening the buttocks muscles. Keep the upper body still and strong. Repeat a total of 6 times, perfecting your form each time. Bring the leg back to its starting position.

don't lean forward

keep hips stacked

5a Keeping the left leg slightly elevated, rotate it again, turning the foot and knee up to the ceiling. Inhale and kick the left leg high in one swift movement. Aim the leg for a spot just behind the ear as you kick up.

rotate the top leg open

keep chest high

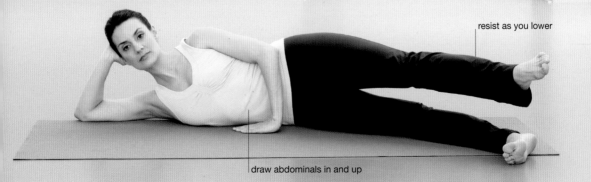

5b Lower your leg down, creating resistance as you go, for a count of 3. Use opposition: as your leg lowers, your abdominals should draw inward and upward. Lift your chest as you repeat 5 more times—for a total of 6 repetitions.

resist as you lower

draw abdominals in and up

from the bottom up >>

>> **side kicks circles**

6a Remain lying on your side. Carry the top leg just in front of the bottom leg. It should feel very heavy at this point. Keep it rotated up to the sky with the ankle long.

keep eyes ahead

keep front heel facing down

6b Draw 10 tiny circles with the leg in the air without shaking your body. Pause briefly. Switch immediately, taking the left leg back and reversing the circles. Keep the circles tiny and emphasize the downward portion of the circle. Repeat 10 circles and pause before resting the left leg on the right.

keep shoulders down

feel it here

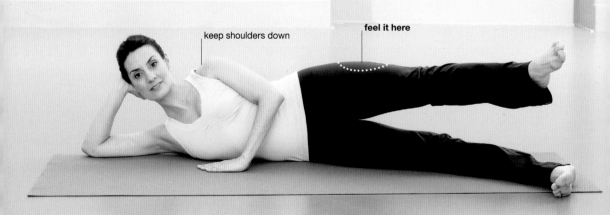

side kicks inner-thigh lifts

7a Remain lying on your right side. Cross the left leg in front of the right leg and take hold of the ankle. Place the left foot flat on the floor with the knee and foot pointing down toward the bottom foot. Now, flex the right foot and lift the entire right leg just above the mat.

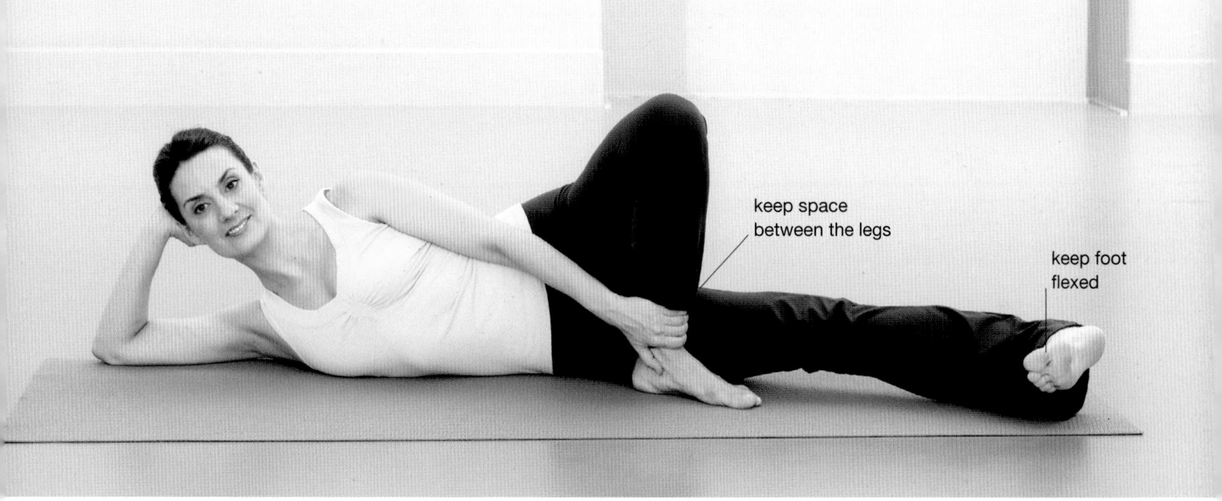

keep space
between the legs
keep foot
flexed

7b Without hunching or collapsing, raise the right leg to its highest point and lower it back to above the mat. Repeat 7 more times for a total of 8 repetitions. On the last repetition, remain at the highest point and perfect the position by lengthening, straightening, and rotating just a little bit more. Finally, lower the leg with control.

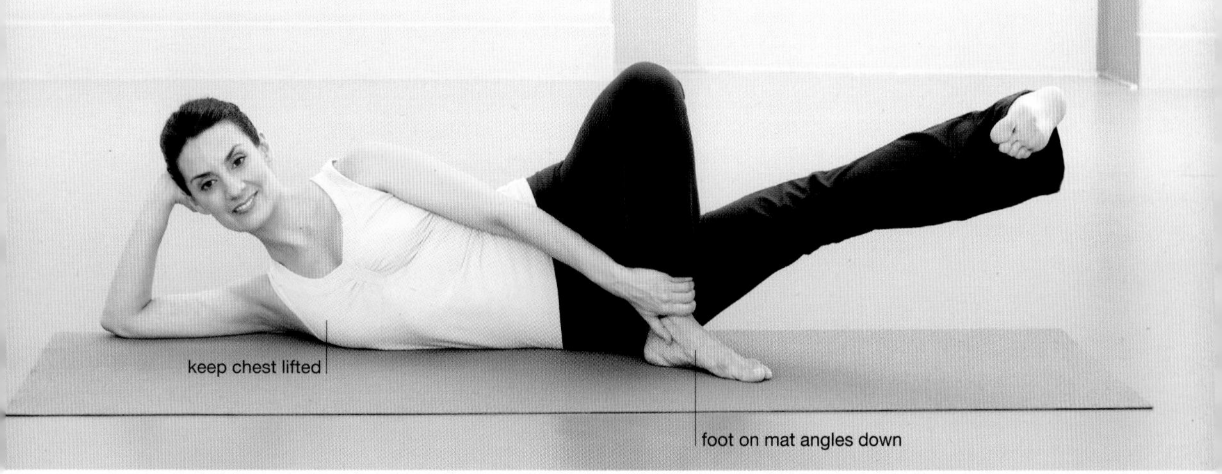

keep chest lifted
foot on mat angles down

>> **side kicks bicycle**

8a Lie with the legs together at a 45° angle in front of you. Raise the left leg slightly. Swing it out in front of the body without hunching or rounding the back. Create opposition by pulling back, or retracting, the left hip behind you slightly. Bend the left knee in toward the shoulder.

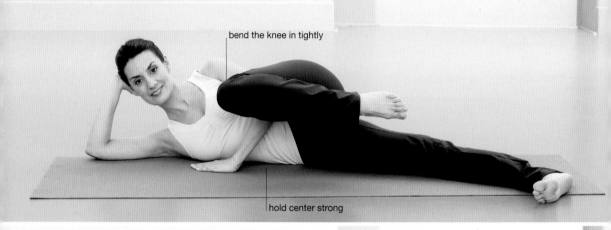

bend the knee in tightly

hold center strong

8b Sweep the left knee down next to the right knee before extending it behind you. Pull the waist up in opposition to the leg reaching down. Repeat 2 more times and then return the leg to its start position. Reverse direction for 3 more repetitions.

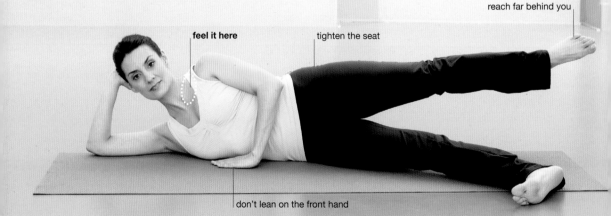

reach far behind you

feel it here   tighten the seat

don't lean on the front hand

>> **from the bottom up**

>> beats on stomach

9a Transition onto your stomach, then lie face down on your mat. Place your hands under your forehead and stretch your legs out. Tighten your abdominals and elevate both legs slightly. Keep your shoulders pulling back and down as you open your legs and start to beat them together.

draw shoulders down

lift knees off mat

9b Breathing naturally, continue beating briskly for 20 counts. Beat the legs from the upper inner thighs and keep the knees straight. Pause at the end to lengthen the legs, tighten the abs, and soften the neck and shoulders, before lowering the legs with control. Roll over onto the other side and repeat the Side Kick series (Steps 3a–8b) with the opposite leg.

beat inner thighs together

keep knees off floor

from the bottom up >>

>> **the teaser**

10a Transition onto your back and bring your knees into your chest as you reach your arms overhead.

keep ribs in

take arms in line with ears

10b In one count, sweep your body up to sitting, balancing with your legs at 90°, arms reaching forward, abs deeply scooped, chest open. With control, curl your tail under you, laying your spine onto the mat. Fold your knees in, arms overhead to repeat. Perform 5 repetitions.

reach beyond legs

scoop abs in

11a Sit cross-legged with your arms open to the side as though you were holding a weight in each hand. Angle your arms so they slope down from shoulders to elbows to wrists. Press your shoulders down and elongate your neck. Feel that your arms are heavy.

tense arm muscle

lengthen sides of waist

11b Inhale and hug with the arms, creating a huge circle in front of you. Exhale and open the arms with even greater resistance. Repeat 3 times, then reverse the breathing for 3 more repetitions. Keep the abdominals pulled inward throughout.

keep neck long

draw shoulders down

>> **the mermaid**

12a Sit to the right side of your legs with your knees, shins, and ankles stacked on your left. Reach your left hand underneath your bottom ankle and hook onto it, holding firmly. Sweep your free right arm up overhead and inhale to prepare.

lengthen waist

hold the bottom ankle firmly

12b Bend lightly over the legs, exhaling as you stretch the right side. Reach the arm and body higher up as you return to upright. Repeat 2 more times, pausing at the end, lifting the waist, and pulling the shoulders down. Swing the legs to the other side for 3 more repetitions.

reach up and over

open elbow out

13a Stand in Pilates stance. Shift your weight slightly forward. Hold your arms by your thighs with your palms facing forward. Inhale, then exhale and raise your arms straight up to the sky.

13b Flip the palms outward and circle the arms down, exerting pressure as though the air were thick. Repeat 2 more times, then reverse the breath, inhaling on the raise and exhaling on the lower, for another 3 repetitions.

palms face back

take arms slightly forward

resist as you lower

lean slightly forward

4a

▲ **Side Kicks Front** page 196

page 195

4b

▲ **Side Kicks Front** page 196

10a

▲ **The Teaser** page 202

page 201

10b

▲ **The Teaser** page 202

summary from the bottom up

▲ Pilates Stance 1 page 194

2

▲ Pilates Stance 2 page 194

3a
▲ Side Kicks Preparation page 195

3b
▲ Side Kicks Preparatio

8a
▲ Side Kicks Bicycle 200

8b
▲ Side Kicks Bicycle page 200

9a
▲ Beats on Stomach page 201

9b
▲ Beats on Stomac

from the bottom up >>

5 minute **summary**

7a

7b

▲ **Side Kicks Inner-thigh Lifts** page 199

s page 198

▲ **Side Kicks Inner-thigh Lifts** page 199

12b

13a

13b

▲ **The Mermaid** page 204

▲ **Arm Circles** page 205

▲ **Arm Circles** page 205

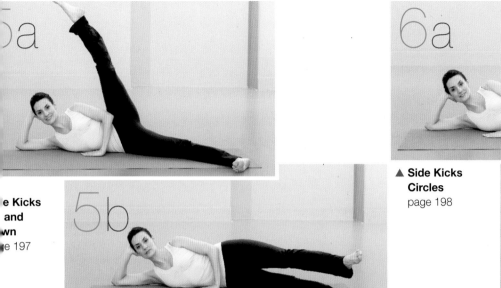

5a

6a

▲ **Side Kicks
Circles**
page 198

6b

e Kicks
and
wn
e 197

5b

▲ **Side Kicks Up and Down** page 197

▲ **Side Kicks Circle**

1a

12a

e Hug
e 203

11b

▲ **The Hug** page 203

▲ **The Mermaid** page 204

>> **from the bottom up** extras

Remember the old style workouts like calisthenics? The Bottom Up program looks eerily similar. The critical difference is precision and form. Focus on controlling your movements rather than hurling your body around. You'll accomplish both form and function at the same time.

>> ## Checklist

Every portion of every exercise is equally important. If you believe you've mastered a move, look again.

• Did you work with opposition, lengthening the torso against the limbs and vice versa?

• Have you focused on what the top half of the body is doing during this lower-body series?

• Can you incorporate your Pilates Stance exercises into the rest of the mat exercises, even when the legs are in the air?

• During Pilates Stance 2, could you feel with your hands that your rotation muscles were pulling the legs into position?

• The Side Kicks focus so heavily on the lower body that people forget their upper bodies. Did you keep your chest lifted and shoulders down throughout?

• For the Side Kicks Front and the Side Kicks Circles, did you maintain your torso alignment without rolling onto the front hand when the leg traveled behind you?

• When you are performing the Beats on Stomach, can you actively draw your shoulder blades down and together in order to avoid hunching and to keep the chest open?

>> Modify/Adjust

Remember, to decrease the intensity you must draw your limbs closer to your center. If you must bend them, go ahead.

• Change the leg position into parallel if the rotation of the hips is too intense during the Side Kicks.

• Alter your position to separate your legs for the Mermaid instead of allowing your shins to rest against one another.

>> Challenge

Experiment with your own positions. A slight pivot or angle change can alter an exercise dramatically.

• Learn to anchor the bottom leg while you are performing the Side Kicks series to increase your stability.

• Attempt to perform the Teaser with legs extended at a 45° angle as you rise up and as you lower.

• Try to add light ankle weights to the Side Kicks if the exercises become too easy.

• Switch the hand on the mat to behind the head for the Side Kicks series. Keep your elbow pointing to the sky.

>> Trainer tips

Use your eyes to position your legs where they look the best, then work from there, making sure the muscles look taut and shapely.

• I constructed the Pilates Stance exercises to provide a support system for much of the work we do in the Pilates method, so practice those regularly. Remember to initiate from your hips.

• This Teaser version is my own and is meant to eliminate self-doubt and to work the core. Remember to focus on the descent.

• It's a good idea to trick your body every now and then by starting on a different side. If you typically begin your leg series on the right, alternate on certain days to begin with the left. Similarly, if you find that you sit cross-legged with the right leg on top all the time, make a change every now and then.

15 minute

Focus on flow
Activate opposition and integration
Learn the standing routine

up, up,
and away >>

>> **up, up,** and away

This last program establishes the muscle memory you will need to set you up for everyday life. We often need to bend, twist, lean, and reach—all moves you will perform here. Your ultimate goal is to subconsciously incorporate your Pilates practice into every waking moment for a stronger, safer body.

The program begins with two seated exercises that help with those all-too-common neck misalignments. We follow these with a challenging variation of the Hundred and some classic Pilates Rowing exercises. Then it's onto our knees for some more classic exercises that reinforce our use of internal resistance. When we come up to standing, we will perform some historical Pilates exercises to strengthen our lower limbs.

Starting and finishing

As you begin the Neck Strengthener, take a minute to fix your posture. Your neck is an extension of your spine and it will be impossible to align your neck if your spine is rounded over. Take note of the top of your head where it begins to slope downward in a curve. This is the crown of the head. As you sit, stand, kneel, or lie, you should always be reaching the crown of the head up and away from you.

You end with the Sides Splits—a functional exercise group. By training your body to engage your core during these dynamic moving exercises, you are preparing for the unexpected movements that you will encounter in real life. Here, focus on your waistline pulling up and away from your legs as you drag the legs together each time.

Transitions

Transfer in controlled, neat movements from the opening neck exercises to the seated movements. To transition to kneeling, tuck your knees into your

> >> **secrets** of success
>
> - **Many find the Chest Expansion** rather subtle. Remember to activate your powerhouse and pull the arms behind you as you turn your head.
>
> - **When you kneel** during the Thigh Stretch, tighten all your muscles from top to tail. You should lock your body as though it were a piece of steel.
>
> - **The Footwork series** are historical Pilates moves. These squatlike movements require full-body integration.

body and then bring them underneath you, raising up your torso as you do so. When it's time to stand, you need only to place your hands on the mat, tuck your toes underneath you, and roll up to standing. As you move from one exercise in the Footwork series to the next, pay special attention to the alignment of your upper body. No matter how you get there, using symmetrical efficient movement without expending excess energy should be your goal.

Up, Up, and Away will reinforce the total-body integration of Pilates. Prepare your body for everyday life by taking the philosophy of Pilates with you everywhere.

>> neck press/shoulder roll

keep elbow open

keep hips relaxed

1 Sit cross-legged and place one hand behind your head. Draw your chin in and slightly down, thereby pressing your skull back toward your hand. Your neck will lengthen and your waist will draw inward. Meet the resistance of your head with your hand and hold for 3 counts. Release gently. Repeat 4 more times for a total of 5 repetitions.

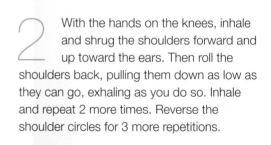

squeeze shoulder blades close

2 With the hands on the knees, inhale and shrug the shoulders forward and up toward the ears. Then roll the shoulders back, pulling them down as low as they can go, exhaling as you do so. Inhale and repeat 2 more times. Reverse the shoulder circles for 3 more repetitions.

hold abs tight

sit very tall

3a
Sit upright with your legs in front of you. Reach your arms over your legs and draw your waistline in and up. Press your shoulders down firmly and begin pumping your arms briskly up and down, breathing in for 5 counts and out for 5.

keep the abs working

3b
Continue pumping as you squeeze the legs and buttocks muscles tight. Hold the body strong so as not to bounce or sway. When you reach 100 pumps or 10 breath cycles, sit taller. Hold for one final moment, then rest.

pump the arms

hold legs together tightly

>> rowing 1

4a Holding the small hand weights, sit tall with your legs extended forward and pressed together. Bend your elbows and pull them behind you to tuck the weights in by your sides. Inhale and extend your arms up without allowing your shoulders to rise.

press shoulders down

keep ankles long

4b Exhale and lower your arms straight down by your hips. Inhale and lift them up overhead again. Now, reach higher and open your arms sideways, circling them down to begin again. Tuck them in, and repeat twice more for a set of 3 repetitions.

rise up as arms lower

lift chest high

5a Sit tall with your legs extended, feet flexed, and holding the weights by your hips. Inhale and round over your legs. Exhale and press your hands forward along the mat toward your feet. Keep your abs lifted. Inhale and roll up through your spine to sitting, reaching your arms over your legs.

take shoulders over hips

press heels forward

circle arms within peripheral vision

5b Continue reaching the arms forward and then take them up to the sky. Circle the arms down and around by your sides to begin again. Repeat a total of 3 times.

press legs together

>> **spine twist**

6a Sit tall with your legs pressed together in front of you and your arms reaching directly over them. Keep your hands reaching long and your feet flexed. Inhale to prepare and lift your waist. Feel the top of your head lengthening up to the sky.

keep chest lifted

keep thighs tight

6b Exhale and twist right, taking the right arm backward and rising up in the torso simultaneously. Make another small twist, then rebound to your starting position. Repeat to the left. Perform 4 sets for a total of 8 repetitions, opposing the arms strongly with every twist.

press back
shoulder down

reach front
arm forward

feel it here

feel it here

7a Open the arms side to side, palms face down. Open the legs just past mat-width. Flex the feet and lift up tall to begin. Inhale and twist to the right, keeping the hips and legs planted firmly on the mat.

grow tall as you twist

take legs hip-width apart

7b Turn your head to follow your back arm. Dive forward, reaching your left hand outside your right foot as though you were sawing off your little toe. Continue to exhale and stretch. Return upright and repeat, twisting to the left. Complete 3 full sets, alternating sides.

let head hang

feel it here

reach past the little toe

>> lotus

8a Take your weights and kneel upright on your mat with your knees comfortably apart. Your arms extend to the sides of your body with the palms face up. Hold strong in your core and keep your chest lifted.

8b Without disrupting your posture, raise the arms straight up, framing the head and neck in an oval. Lower the arms back down with controlled resistance. Keep the elbows soft. Repeat for a total of 8 times, exhaling to lift and inhaling to lower.

keep arms within peripheral vision

hold buttocks tight

take arms in line with ears

keep spine aligned

9a Still kneeling upright, hold the weights just in front of you. Tighten the buttocks and pull up in the waist to activate the core. Inhale and sweep the arms behind you with resistance, opening the chest and drawing the shoulder blades together as you go.

9b Keep the arms behind you as you look over the right shoulder and then the left before returning to center. Exhale and take the arms back in front of you. Repeat 3 more times, alternating the initial direction you turn the head with each set.

retract shoulder blades

lift chest high

stretch your neck

work the powerhouse

>> **thigh stretch**

10a Remain on your knees holding the weights with your arms extended directly in front of you just below shoulder-height. Face your palms down and tighten your powerhouse to begin. Inhale to prepare.

10b Allow your chin to dip down slightly then hinge back, stretching the fronts of your thighs but not arching your spine. At your lowest point, tighten your buttocks and bring your body back up to start again. Perform a total of 4 repetitions, exhaling each time you rise back up. Put the weights down. Tuck your toes under you to come up to standing.

don't round shoulders

keep weight even over legs

keep eyes level with horizon

feel it here

tighten seat

11 Come off your mat and stand up tall in Pilates stance. Place your hands behind your head, elbows wide. Inhale and bend your knees to lower into a squat. Allow your heels to rise. At the bottom of the squat, press your heels into the floor to rise back up. Perform 6 times, inhaling to lower and exhaling to rise.

12 Stand with feet parallel, hip-width apart, arms folded in front of you at chest height. Bend your knees as low as you can go, then push your feet into the floor to rise. Repeat for 6 repetitions. Inhale to lower and exhale to rise.

keep spine upright

heels rise and lower

keep chest lifted

reach knees forward

anchor heels down

13 Standing with feet together and arms extended in front for stability, curl the toes up and press the rest of the foot firmly down. Pull the abs in, then bend into a squat. Keep the heels down if possible and stay as upright as you can, resisting the urge to bend too far forward in the spine. Exhale to rise back up with resistance. Don't rush. Repeat a total of 6 times.

14 Return to Pilates stance, with your arms folded in front at chest height. Press down firmly into the floor with the balls of your feet so your heels rise up for 3 counts. Lower down with control. Continue for 6 repetitions exhaling as you rise and inhaling as you lower.

don't lean back

keep buttocks tight

send hips back

squeeze inner thighs

lift toes high

15 Once again, stand in Pilates stance, arms out to your sides. Lunge forward with your left leg, transferring all your weight onto it. Keep your right leg firmly planted into the floor. Drag your left foot back to the right foot to start again. Inhale to lunge and exhale to pull back 4 times on each leg.

16 Return to Pilates stance, with the arms reaching out to the sides. Lunge sideways with the left leg, then drag the leg home, straightening it as quickly as possible to activate the upper inner thighs. Repeat 3 more times. Repeat with the other leg to the side.

eep shoulders down

keep arms within peripheral vision

lift your waist

feel it here

make sure muscles of inner thighs are working

4a

▲ **Rowing 1**
page 220

4b

219

▲ **Rowing 1** page 220

9b

10a

10b

▲ **Chest Expansion** page 225

▲ **Thigh Stretch** page 226

▲ **Thigh Stretch** page 226

ck Press
e 218

▲ **The Hundred** page 219

▲ **Shoulder Roll** page 218

▲ The Hundred pag

us page 224

▲ **Lotus** page 224

▲ **Chest Expansion** page 225

up, up, and away

5 minute **summary**

▲ **The Saw**
page 223

▲ **The Saw** page 223

▲ **Tendon Stretch** page 228   ▲ **Front Splits** page 229   ▲ **Side Splits** page 229

Rowing 2
page 221

▲ **Spine Twist**
page 222

▲ **Rowing 2** page 221

▲ **Spine Twist** page

▲twork 1 page 227

▲ **Footwork 2** page 227

▲ **Footwork 3** page 228

>> **up, up, and away** extras

Consider the pace of your everyday life. Do you ever have time truly to prepare for a movement, a reach, or a shift of your weight? Not likely. Life happens fast. The ideal exercise routine will prepare you for that speed. Use this routine to prepare for your regular day.

>> Checklist

As you work through this program, be certain not to limit your attention to one area of the body. All of your muscles should work.

• Did you focus on your posture for the whole program?

• Have you established the feeling of making space between your vertebrae to elongate your spine?

• Can you feel the level of work required in the waistline and the fatigue it can cause to sit up tall?

• Were you able to keep your inner thighs drawn together and the legs zipped up during the Hundred?

• For the Rowing 1 exercise, the torso is challenged to remain vertical while the arms sweep up and down. Did you manage to initiate the movement from your core to keep your body stable?

• Opening the back arm during the Spine Twist is fairly simple, but turning the whole opposite side of the rib cage to the front is tough. Were you able to spiral around your own spine, lifting taller throughout the torso the whole time?

• At the most intense portion of the Thigh Stretch, where your body is hinged backward, were you able to tighten your buttocks to create even more stretch in the front of the thighs?

• Timing is everything in the Footwork series. Rather than rushing your body through moves, slowing down slightly will increase the work to your muscles and have a greater benefit.

>> Modify/Adjust

Adding weights to your program can be a challenge. Practice the exercises without the weights before adding them.

• Soften the knees or sit cross-legged for any seated exercises that cause strain in straight-legged positions.

• Reduce the depth of the knee bends for Footwork 1, 2, and 3.

• Place a cushion under you to protect your knees when kneeling.

• Take your hands across the chest or behind the head as you perform the Spine Twist, to reduce the range.

>> Challenge

Remember, if the exercise doesn't seem challenging, you aren't working hard enough. Review the details and try again.

• Remember, continuously feel the top of your head growing higher up during Rowing 1 and 2.

• Learn to stretch a bit deeper in the Saw—coming up only after you've gone as far as possible.

• Train yourself to work the inner thighs tirelessly whenever seated with the legs together, as in Rowing 1 and 2.

• Try to exaggerate the opposition in twisting or rotary movements.

>> Trainer tips

Be mindful that your center of gravity and balance will change as you rise up through different positions.

• Our bodies follow a developmental sequence from birth to childhood, moving from lying to sitting, kneeling, and, finally, standing. This program takes you through that sequence but gives you the opportunity to check your symmetry.

• When performing the Footwork series, the rising up with control is the hardest movement. Rather than try to get up away from the floor, think of boring a hole into the floor with your feet. The harder you push down, the more the floor will push up against you.

• The Front and Side Splits mirror with the limbs what's going on internally. Envision your muscles pulling inward and upward as the legs pull together.

15 minute

Focus on consistency
Activate proper body mechanics
Learn the story of Pilates

beyond the
workout >>

>> **workout** schedule

Pilates is meant to be accessible, attainable, and convenient. Whether it's 15 minutes three times a week or 45 minutes every day to devote to your daily fitness, the pilates workouts in this book can be structured to suit your schedule. Below are three programs to start you off.

If you only have 15 minutes a day three times a week, simply rotate the four programs, choosing a different one each day until you've cycled through all four and are ready to begin again. If you can squeeze in between 15 and 30 minutes per day, the Day by Day workout should be done on alternating days three days per week to emphasize and develop the core of the body. On Tuesdays and Thursdays you will get to test how well you can integrate the main principles and positions in the other three programs in an extended 30-minute workout. If you can manage 30 to 45 minutes a day, I recommend performing the Day by Day workout every day and following up with alternating programs, choosing one day as your longest workout day.

>> **pilates** workout planner

	Available time 15 minutes, 3 times a week	15–30 minutes a day	30–45 minutes a day
Monday	Day by Day (week 1) Up, Up, and Away (week 2) From the Bottom Up (week 3)	Day by Day	Day by Day From the Top Down
Tuesday		Up, Up, and Away From the Top Down	Day by Day Up, Up, and Away
Wednesday	From the Top Down (week 1) Day by Day (week 2) Up, Up, and Away (week 3)	Day by Day	Day by Day From the Bottom Up From the Top Down
Thursday		From the Bottom Up Up, Up, and Away	Day by Day Up, Up, and Away
Friday	From the Bottom Up (week 1) From the Top Down (week 2) Day by Day (week 3)	Day by Day	Day by Day From the Bottom Up

Built-in flexibility

There is a high degree of flexibility in this series. You can decide to do one program each day or all four if you choose. In the beginning, it is always wise to ease in slowly, limiting your day to one or two programs. After two or three weeks, you can attempt a longer routine.

To help keep you on track, be sure to plan actively for your workout. I recommend that you make a note of your workout in your planner so that it is given just as much importance as all your other obligations. Remember that your health and wellness should always take center stage in your life.

If there are days you just can't get to your workout, read about it, or watch the DVD. Either way, studying a physical method without engaging has an astounding benefit. You could actually improve your form, elevate your technique, and refine your practice, even without performing the workout. This phenomenon is known as physiological empathy and although it won't build muscle mass or shrink your waist, you can learn and improve significantly by keen observation alone.

Take time to learn about your workout. Simply looking at images and reading about the exercises you do will actually help you improve your practice significantly.

>> **after** the workout

When I attend fitness events I am always amused by a particular phenomenon. After their workouts, and at the first opportunity, students revert quickly to their poor posture and slink out of the room with stooped shoulders, sunken chests, and protruding midsections. Not so with Pilates.

In your 15-minute Pilates routines you have been required to build stamina in your postural muscles. The muscles surrounding your spine and running alongside it from your tail to your head have been called upon to perform throughout. Sadly for this particular group of muscles, unless you are lying on your back, they don't get to rest. By working on these postural muscles you are in a better position to employ body mechanics after your workout. When they count the most!

This doesn't mean that poor body mechanics won't resurface occasionally. I am sympathetic to the pull of bad habits. I personally descend from poor posture lineage. For instance, something terrible happens when your body assumes a seated position. All muscle activity arrests. To combat this state of muscle inertia, be sure to leave your chair at regular intervals. At minimum, stand up and reach overhead, stretching your body. Sustained inactivity is unnatural and damaging. When a hospital patient is bedridden, it takes only 12 hours of immobility for bedsores to begin to form. Movement and blood flow are vital to life.

If you are working out and then returning to work, take advantage of the jolt of energy you get immediately after your workout. Rather than revert to a sedentary role, try to keep moving as long as possible. If you commute after your workout, stand for some portion of the trip so your muscles have time to adjust. If you must sit, take the opportunity to work on your sitting posture. Try to keep the chest lifted and the abdominals supported.

Sit up straight! Once you return to your normal activities, remember to maintain your spinal alignment. Good sitting posture will improve your internal organ function and increase your energy levels.

Stretching

Stretching is good for the body, but never before your workout. Cutting-edge research shows that this is detrimental! Your strength is dramatically reduced as your muscles simply shut off in response. This is not to say you shouldn't stretch. By all means, do. But do so after your workout when your stretching will have the most benefit.

There is always one person in my class stretching away in a straddle position, bobbing up and down trying to get a deeper stretch. Nothing could be less effective. This "ballistic stretching" actually causes your muscles to contract even tighter. Only by sustained static stretching, that is, holding the stretch completely still and relaxing into it, will you become more flexible. This is the only method of increasing tissue extensibility. If you don't have time to stretch after your workout, do some simple stretches after your shower when your muscles are sufficiently heated.

Soreness

As with any effective training regimen, some soreness is normal. It is caused by micro-tears in the muscle fiber but the good news is that, as the muscle rebuilds, it reshapes into a toned, sculpted, and slightly larger version of its former self.

Pilates soreness often occurs two days after a workout and not the very next day. To help alleviate it, make sure to hydrate before you start your workout. On days that you do feel muscle aches, the best remedy is movement. It sounds unlikely, I know. Most people think that you should rest if you feel sore, but by flushing blood through the painful areas you are restoring balance to your system and quickening your healing process. Whenever possible you should perform a few Pilates moves on days that you feel the most sore.

Stretch it out! Stretching should be done only after your workout—never before. This simple hamstring stretch can be done anywhere you can prop up your foot. Simply keep your hips square and your chest lifted. Place your hands on your thigh and gently lean into the stretch.

>> **motivation** tools

Exercise will help you get through your daily life, but life offers you cues to motivate your exercise. If you want to go higher, faster, better, exercise will help you. Mr. Pilates understood that motivation is cumulative. He said begin with just 10 minutes a day. That small start can have far-reaching effects.

One of my favorite Pilates quotes is "Physical fitness can neither be obtained through outright purchase nor wishful thinking." Overcoming the psychological barriers to exercise can be daunting. Here are a few alternative thoughts to ignite your exercise impulse:

It takes energy to make energy: You will feel more awake, not more tired, after you exercise.
Exercise only works as hard as you do: If you feel low on energy, work out lightly. You do not have to push yourself to the limit each time you work out. It's all right to take it easy on some days.
A workout isn't work: Think of your fitness regimen as a luxury. It's maintenance for sure, but it's not a chore for your body; it's more like dessert!

Staying motivated

Here are a couple of my favorite tips for staying motivated that are culled from my clients and staff members:
Rewards: Do something nice for yourself for every week you complete your workout regimen. For instance, have a manicure, buy tickets for an event.
Reality check: Cut yourself some slack. Simply performing the exercise is enough. If you don't have the energy to put extra effort into it, it will still be beneficial.
Rhythm: It's taboo in the Pilates world, but if you're sure that music will unleash your inner Pilates superhero, then go for it. Put on your favorite mix of tunes and get started.
Reinforcement: If you like a certain exercise, do

> >> **tips to** help your practice
>
> - **Rhythm counts.** Remember to work out at the rhythm of your heart. As you get better, your workout should get shorter and faster.
>
> - **Live Pilates!** Use your Pilates in everyday life to keep you symmetrical and well aligned; stand on equal footing instead of leaning to one side; sit with your ankles crossed instead of your knees; walk with generous strides, leading with your hips as you go.
>
> - **Make a Pact!** Create a support system with a friend to make sure you keep on track no matter what.

some extra ones during the day. You can also take a moment to show someone else how good you are at it. Positive reinforcement goes a long way toward motivation.

Buddy up

Studies show that people who work out with a friend work out longer and harder. Plan to do Pilates with someone and then police each other so you don't fall off the wagon. It's infinitely harder to turn down a friend than just to skip out on yourself. And a bit of competition among friends can also be very inspiring. Finally, try teaching a friend some of the moves you've learned. Teaching is very often a learning process. As you dissect and explain the exercises to someone else, you will be absorbing information for your own body.

Be committed

Experts say it takes 21 days to build a new habit. You won't see a change after one workout, but you will feel it! Commit to 21 days of this. Grab a calendar and check off the days. I expect that by the last few days you won't be counting down any more. You'll be counting up instead—counting the increased number of repetitions you are able to perform, the longer workout you're able to get through and, finally, the hours to go until your next great workout.

Complementary workouts

I suggest swimming, weight-training, and yoga to complement Pilates: swimming for its nonimpact cardiovascular benefits; weight-training to increase bone density and your metabolic rate; yoga for its quiet and stillness. The caveat here is: mix it up. Your body will accommodate to training benefits over time and so it is important to change things around periodically. Whatever other type of training you choose, be certain you incorporate all of your Pilates principles. And remember, the best exercise you can do is the one that you enjoy!

Don't go it alone! Change your exercise routine and take a friend along with you. Instead of going out for a coffee, work out together.

>> **the story** of pilates

Fitness fads come and go. New exercise systems crop up and disappear overnight. Few stand the test of time. Pilates formally established his method in the 1920s and today his system of body conditioning is stronger than ever. Worldwide, some 10 million people practice Pilates. Clearly, Pilates works!

So many versions of the Pilates history exist side by side, it can be hard to weed out the truth. But sometimes it's easier to discern what isn't true than to look for what is. Here are some of the common myths about Pilates debunked.

• **Pilates is for dancers.** False. Pilates is certainly enjoyed by dancers. But Joseph Pilates did not have a specific audience in mind when he was devising his system.
• **Pilates was a dancer.** No. Joseph Pilates was many things—a diver, gymnast, boxer, and acrobat, but he was never a dancer.
• **Pilates is a stretching technique.** No. But every exercise has a lengthening component. A Pilates session can certainly be tailored to address muscular tightness but this is not its sole focus.
• **Pilates requires machines.** Yes. And no. The Pilates Mat work is a total body workout requiring no apparatus. To do the entire Pilates system, one must find a studio with the proper equipment.
• **Pilates is a woman's workout.** Absolutely not. Joseph Pilates did not invent his method for women. In fact, these days men are reclaiming Pilates and there are more male instructors available than ever.

The man

Joseph Pilates was born in 1880 near Dusseldorf in a town called Mönchengladbach. His parents were in the health and fitness fields, his father having been a gymnast and his mother, a naturopath.

To dear Mary-
from uncle
Joe
1947.

Joseph Pilates was a fitness pioneer who borrowed from ancient disciplines and modern technology to create an entirely new system of body conditioning.

Despite a rocky start as a frail, sickly boy, the young Pilates became passionate about anatomy and movement, and studied yoga as well as Zen and ancient Greek and Roman training regimens. As a result, by the age of 14, he was in extraordinary shape and began to model for anatomy charts.

In reading through the things Joseph Pilates said and his history, it becomes evident that he was indeed a visionary. And that was by no means limited to exercise. One could argue that, with his invention of the Wunda Chair—meant to function as furniture when not used for exercise—he created the first home gym. He also recorded an infomercial of sorts, showing his work and machines to the public. He routinely photographed his clients before and after exercise, to record their dramatic results. Were he alive today, Pilates would be up-to-date with his marketing strategies. Sadly for him, he did not realize the success of his method in his lifetime.

One of his greatest dreams was to see his method practiced in schools worldwide. In the United States today, there is a movement underway and several schools have adopted the system.

The machines

Although Mr. Pilates began with his system of floor exercises, he did turn his attention toward the invention of apparatus specifically for his method. His inspiration came from various sources and there is no limit to the tales that surround his creativity. For example, it is often told that Pilates created his Magic Circle (an original thighmaster if you will) from the steel bands of beer kegs. How he came to invent his larger spring-driven equipment was a result of his internship on the Isle of Man during World War I. Pilates was training his captive comrades, many of whom were bedridden. At the

time, hospital beds were constructed with springs so Mr. Pilates began to experiment by attaching these springs to the posts of the beds, thereby providing assistance to weakened muscles.

This particular device went through several transformations and is known in the modern Pilates world as the Cadillac or sometimes as the Trapeze Table. In addition, Pilates created a wooden frame with a sliding carriage and variable springs that outperformed his other inventions in terms of variety and accessibility. He labeled this apparatus the Universal Reformer. The Universal Reformer is by far the most commonly used apparatus today and can be found in most, if not all, dedicated Pilates studios around the world.

By the time of his death in 1967, Mr. Pilates had created several dozen distinct apparatuses to accompany his tremendous library of exercises.

The method

Today, Pilates is everywhere—in people's homes, on TV, and in the gyms. The method is available in some form or other at fitness facilities worldwide. There are fusions, hybrids, and cross-training models, all of which are based either fully or in part on the Pilates method.

The Pilates tradition is being passed on to myriad teachers via the five remaining students of Joseph Pilates himself. These master teachers have dedicated their lives to teaching and have passed on their versions, thereby continuing the evolution of the work. Yet, as the method grows, it will become increasingly important to preserve the original work so that the material retains integrity.

What Pilates was or is becoming is less important than what Pilates is to you today. If you experience Pilates as I do, as a comprehensive workout, which delivers the strength, stability, and mobility necessary for overall health, then there is simply no reason not to do it.

Shown in a studio setting, a row of Universal Reformers, as they are made today. It is the most commonly used Pilates apparatus worldwide.

useful resources

The Pilates method has grown tremendously in recent years and, as a result, hundreds of products are now available to the consumer. Use discretion when choosing Pilates products and be sure to verify the company's credibility and experience with the method. I have listed some reliable sources for all things Pilates-related below.

Other books by Alycea Ungaro

Pilates: Body in Motion
(Dorling Kindersley, 2002)
The original resource for the complete Mat repertoire including leveled workouts for beginner, intermediate, and advanced exercisers.

The Pilates Promise
(Dorling Kindersley, 2004)
Joseph Pilates made a guarantee that he could give you a whole new body in 30 sessions. Alycea tests his promise with three different women and charts their progress and amazing results.

Pilates Body in Motion Flashcards
(Dorling Kindersley, 2007)
Based on the book, these flashcards are designed for easy portability. Take your favorite exercises with you.

Portable Pilates™ (Pilates Center of New York, 2000)
With user-friendly illustrations, spiral binding, and a 38-minute audio workout on CD, this Pilates set is a great primer to take on your travels.

Books by Joseph Pilates

From the master himself, these two resources boast the virtues of exercise and criticize the sedentary lifestyle that has been imposed on us by civilization.

Return to Life through Contrology
(Bodymind Publishing Inc.,1998)
Learn the classic Mat exercises as demonstrated by Joseph Pilates. The complete original Mat work is presented in this historic text.

Your Health
(Presentation Dynamics, 1998)
With recommendations ranging from dry-brushing to proper breathing, this is Mr. Pilates' essay on total wellness.

Audio downloads

Exercise should go where you do. The internet now offers a host of options for accessible exercise.

www.iAmplify.com
Bringing together fitness and lifestyles, iAmplify offers material you can simply load directly onto your desktop, mp3, or iPod for instant accessibility. Log on for live recorded workouts with Alycea.

www.Podfitness.com
Bringing together the top fitness trainers in a variety of disciplines, Podfitness offers you the ability to upload workouts designed by your favorite trainer. Alycea works together with Podfitness to develop Pilates programs suitable for all levels.

Alycea Ungaro's free downloads and Pilates printables
www.realpilatesnyc.com

Pilates blog

If you have exercise questions specific to Pilates or just want to read what others have to say, a blog is a great source for a variety of information.

PilateSpeak

This blog provides a forum for Pilates professionals and students alike. All questions are answered personally by Alycea.

Apparel

Pilates wear is subject to individual requirements and tastes. Some of the companies that cater specifically to the needs of Pilates exercise are listed below.

Lululemon

www.lululemon.com
Functional and fashionable apparel for Pilates.

Marika

www.marika.com
The softest fabrics and clever designs keep the Marika crowd completely loyal to the brand.

Equipment

If you are ready to move on to the next level in your Pilates training and invest in some equipment for your home, try the following manufacturers.

Balanced Body

Produces the entire line of Pilates equipment for home and studio needs.
www.pilates.com

Gratz Pilates

Pilates equipment based on Joseph Pilates' original specifications.
www.pilates-gratz.com

Pilates periodicals

Although there are dozens of fitness magazines, Pilates has relatively few references devoted to the craft.

Pilates Style Magazine

www.pilatesstyle.com

Pilates for special populations

Pilates For Men

The Complete Book of Pilates for Men, Daniel Lyon Jr. (Regan Books, 2005)
This book promises quick and long-term results to any man who seeks optimal fitness and a competitive edge in all aspects of his life.

Post-Pregnancy Pilates, Karrie Adamany (Avery, 2005)
A guide to heal and reshape a new mother's body. How Pilates can change your body after birth.

Classical Pilates Technique in Consideration of the Neck and Back, Peter Fiasca (Classical Pilates, Inc., 2006)
This video demonstrates a progression of safe and educational workouts for the body, attending to today's most common stress-related concerns: neck and back complaints.

For Pilates professionals

Pilates Pro

www.pilates-pro.com
Pilates Pro is an online magazine for all Pilates professionals. It provides the industry with access to vital information, tools, services, and opportunities that promote community and provide teaching and business solutions.

Pilates Method Alliance (PMA)

www.pilatesmethodalliance.org
An international not-for-profit professional association for the Pilates method. The PMA's mission is to protect the public by establishing certification and continuing education standards for Pilates professionals. Find teachers internationally online.

Pilates legacy

Pilates trained many people in his lifetime. Several of them still teach today. It is an honor and a privilege to work with them.

Ron Fletcher
www.ronfletcherwork.com

Kathy Grant
http://dance.tisch.nyu.edu/object/GrantK.html

Romana Kryzanowska
www.romanaspilates.com

Lolita San Miguel
www.lolitapilates.com

Mary Bowen
www.pilates-marybowen.com

index

acknowledgments

Suzanne Martin's acknowledgments

So many thanks to all my teachers, mentors, clients, and students who challenged me to break a movement down into its essence so that I can now pass it on to you. Thanks to my scoliosis and injuries that forced me to find ways to help myself and then to help others. Thanks to DK for being willing to include many concepts and unusual images in this book and to communicate them around the world. A special thanks to Hilary Mandleberg, Jenny Latham, Mary-Clare Jerram, Miranda Fenton, Helen McTeer, Ruth Jenkinson, and Anne Fisher and Susan Downing for their patience, and for working so hard to help me realize my dreams.

Alycea Ungaro's acknowledgments

I was aware during the creation of this project that no task is accomplished alone. I am filled with gratitude for so many people for their constant support, but particularly my mother, Susan Baylis, and my husband, Robert Ungaro, both of whom are responsible for any successes I may have achieved. I want also to thank my delicious girls Emma and Estelle, who tolerated weeks of a busy mommy in the name of this project.

Thanks go to the inimitable publicists of D2 Publicity for making sure the world knows about us, and Laurie Liss @ Sterling Lord Literistic for her agenting prowess. I also thank the beauty squad: Anton Thompson and Mary Schook, as well as Kent Mancini, Victoria Barnes, and Roisin Donaghy. At DK I wish to thank Mary-Clare Jerram, Miranda Harvey, Penny Warren, and Hilary Mandleberg, who understood when the chips were down that long pants were the key to happiness. Shout outs go to the phenomenal team at Alycea Ungaro's Real Pilates, including the instructors who lend me their words and inspiration every day.

Deep and profound appreciation goes out to the administrative team that runs my business and hence my life while I sequester myself to write and create. They are: Casey Kern, (boss of everything), Jan Phillips (ruler of all), and Shelley Hardin (graphics goddess).

I am incredibly thankful to Joel Mishcon for his vision and direction and, of course, to Charlie Arnaldo, who lent her form, eye, and talent to this project and ultimately "made it happen."

Special thanks to Amara Leyton for lending me her mommy, Melody, while I go to work every day, and also to Benjamin and Adeline Teolis for offering their mother, Loren, for hours of phone consultation.

Publisher's acknowledgments

Stretching: Dorling Kindersley thanks photographer Ruth Jenkinson and her assistant Carly Churchill; Viv Riley at Touch Studios; the models Sam Magee and Tara Lee; Rachel Jones for the hair and makeup; sweatyBetty for the loan of exercise clothing; Peter Kirkham for proofreading, and Hilary Bird for the index.

Pilates: Dorling Kindersley thanks photographer Ruth Jenkinson and her assistants, James McNaught and Vic Churchill; sweatyBetty for the loan of the exercise clothing; Viv Riley at Touch Studios; the models Rhona Crewe and Sam Johannesson; Roisin Donaghy and Victoria Barnes for the hair and makeup; YogaMatters for supplying the mat.

Thanks also to Mary Pilates, niece of Joseph Pilates, for her generosity in supplying the photograph of Mr. Pilates on page 246, and to Alycea Ungaro's Real Pilates for the photograph of the Pilates studio on page 247.

about Suzanne Martin

Suzanne is a doctor of physical therapy and a gold-certified Pilates expert. A former dancer, she is a Master trainer certified by the American Council on Exercise. She is published in Dance Magazine, Dance Studio Life, Dorling Kindersley, and the Journal of Dance Medicine and Science, among others. She is also well known within the world of Pilates, dance, and physical therapy. Suzanne is the lead physical therapist for the Smuin Ballet in San Francisco and maintains a private practice, Total Body Development, in Alameda, California.

For more information, check her website www.totalbodydevelopment.com

about Alycea Ungaro

Alycea Ungaro, PT, is the owner of Alycea Ungaro's Real Pilates in New York City and the author of several best-selling Pilates titles including *Portable Pilates™*, *Pilates: Body in Motion*, and *The Pilates Promise*, some of which are available in 17 languages worldwide. Alycea's personal mission is to make Pilates available to everyone regardless of age, fitness level, or geographic location. To that end, Alycea has created Pilates products in every possible medium. She presents seminars and workshops nationally and also serves on the advisory board of *Fitness Magazine*. Alycea is a featured personality on podfitness.com and iamplify.com, where you can download her signature workouts to your desktop or iPod. She lives in New York City with her family. To learn more about Alycea or Alycea Ungaro's Real Pilates, visit www.realpilatesnyc.com

London, New York, Melbourne, Munich, and Delhi

Senior Editor Ros Walford
Jacket Designer Mark Penfound
Production Editor Kavita Varma
Senior Production Controller Kate Blower
Associate Publisher Nigel Duffield

DVDs produced for Dorling Kindersley by
Chrome Productions www.chromeproductions.com

This edition published in 2011
Contains content from *15-Minute Stretching
Workout* (2010) and *15-Minute Everyday Pilates* (2008).

Published in the United States by
DK Publishing, 375 Hudson Street
New York, New York 10014

10 9 8 7 6 5 4 3 2 1

001-184725-Dec/11

Health warning
All participants in fitness activities must assume the
responsibility for their own actions and safety. If you have
any health problems or medical conditions, consult with
your physician before undertaking any of the activities set
out in this book. The information contained in this book
cannot replace sound judgement and good decision
making,which can help reduce risk of injury.

Published in Great Britain by Dorling Kindersley Limited

A catalog record for this book is available from the
Library of Congress

ISBN 978-0-7566-9427-2

DK books are available at special discounts when purchased in bulk
for sales promotions, premiums, fund-raising, or educational use.
For details, contact: DK Publishing Special Markets, 375 Hudson Street,
New York, New York 10014 or SpecialSales@dk.com

Printed and bound in China by Leo Paper Products.

Discover more at
www.dk.com